I0535487

The 100 Watt War

Ron Wilder

Also by Ron Wilder

Aligned Action: The Key to CEO Effectiveness

The 100 Watt War

Ron Wilder

THE 100 WATT WAR

ISBN # 978-0-9835153-3-3

PUBLISHER

Aligned Action, Inc.

3434-135 Kildaire Farm Road, Suite 143

Cary, NC 27518

Printed in the United States of America

COVER DESIGN by Ana Grigoriu, www.anagrigoriu.de

Cover photography of author by Bryan Rierson.

Cover photography of U.S. Capitol by David Iliff.

Stay in touch with the author, follow The 100 Watt War blog, and download an interview with Ron Wilder about the book at: http://www.The100WattWar.com.

First Published in 2012 by Aligned Action, Inc.

TABLE OF CONTENTS

To my grandfathers, George & Charlie, and my dad, Mike.

You guys would have loved this book.

The 100 Watt War

PART I

"History and societies do not crawl. They make jumps. They go from fracture to fracture, with a few vibrations in between."

– Nassim Nicholas Taleb

CHAPTER 1

Mexico, south of the Arizona border.

"¿Quién es?" Who is it? The dark-haired man pressed the intercom button to query the visitor at the front gate of his villa.

"José. Estoy volviendo del supermercado." It's José. I'm returning from the supermarket.

The dark-haired man took a long draw on his cigar as he contemplated this development. Why now? He wondered. He'd been waiting with great anticipation for this day to come for several years. Yet his day to day life had become so routine that he sometimes forgot that it was coming. Then he'd feel guilty when he remembered his real purpose for waiting. But now it was time.

He recalled his lines from a dark corner of his

memory and then spoke into the intercom again. "¿Qué compraste hoy? ¿Pescado o pollo?" What did you buy today? Fish or chicken?

"Ninguno de los dos. Pero he comprado una docena de rosas." Neither. But I did buy a dozen roses.

"¿De qué color? ¿Rojas o rosas?" What color? Red or pink?

"Blancas." White.

"Muy bien. Me gustaría verlas." Very good. I would like to see them.

He silently chuckled at this contrived dance of tradecraft, but did admit that it worked to authenticate his visitor. He pressed a second button which opened the front gate, allowing his visitor's car to pass through. Via the closed-circuit security monitors, he watched the car climb the short hilly road up to the house. As the car approached the circular drive, he opened a garage bay and the car pulled in.

He opened the door from the kitchen into the garage as his guest got out of the car and walked towards him. As they met at the threshold, he took a good look at his visitor. Dark hair, a thick mustache, and scruffy beard growth around the rest of his face. Hazel eyes.

He stepped back to allow his guest inside. The guest carried only a small suitcase and a grocery bag with the white flowers protruding from the top. The guest left the suitcase by the door and set the bag on the table, while the host prepared a large vase for the roses. The guest also pulled out a six-pack of Dos Equis and put it in the fridge, then took off his jacket. The host took the jacket and placed it on a hook behind the door.

With nothing left to put away, the two men stood facing each other in the middle of the kitchen. They looked each other up and down as if meeting their partner in an arranged marriage for the first time. In a sense, that was true. They would be spending all of their time together in the coming months.

Finally the arriving visitor broke the silence.

"Assalamu alaikum." Peace be unto you.

"Wa alaikum assalam wa rahmatu Allah." And to you be peace together with God's mercy.

With this greeting, they embraced and exchanged

light kisses cheek to cheek. As they separated, the host asked "Is it time?"

"Yes, I bring a message and instructions from our leader. But first we must pray."

CHAPTER 2

After they completed the prayers, they rolled up their mats and stowed them in the closet.

"Did you get all of the supplies?" José asked.

"Yes, of course. Everything is prepared as instructed." The host took this opportunity to seek a proper introduction. "José, you are really called Yusef, yes?"

"Shhh. José is all you need to know. I will call you Miguel, as you are already known here. Less risk that way. We must maintain our covers," José replied.

Miguel accepted this explanation for now, yet was still nervous. He'd been preparing for this mission for his entire life and desperately wanted to trust his counterpart. Yet he also knew that he could not ask too many questions without bringing his own loyalty into doubt.

"Come, let's go to the place you've prepared. I will explain more in due time." José sensed Miguel's concern and attempted to put him at ease.

Miguel nodded and led the way to the garage. They got into the car and headed down the road from the villa. He drove towards the small town and then took a right turn to follow a winding road up into the hills.

As he steered through the twists and turns of the road, Miguel wondered about José. He knew that Yusef was legendary within the Al Qaeda ranks because of his expertise in creating detonators to use in improvised explosive devices, or IEDs. One of the key problems of creating effective IEDs is having a reliable detonator. Getting the explosive material is usually easy enough and you can make shrapnel out of ordinary building supplies like nuts and bolts. For the IEDs to work, you needed a good detonator – either a pressure trigger device like a land mine or preferably a remote electronic detonator using something like a cell phone. José had been exceptionally creative in innovating with detonators, which kept them one step ahead of the Americans. Whatever the plan, Miguel figured he was about to learn something really exciting.

About twenty minutes later, they arrived at the end of the road blocked by a large chain link gate. Miguel jumped out of the car, unlocked the padlock, then ran back to the car and drove through the gate and parked next to a large tree. Miguel locked the gate behind them and then showed José into the building – a small warehouse with a single loading dock on one side. The floor of the warehouse was completely open and empty, with only a few machines scattered around the edges of the room. A small pallet sat in one corner with several boxes on top of it. Other than that, the place was bare.

José walked around and inspected. "Looks good. Time to get to work."

José motioned to Miguel. As Miguel walked over, José pulled out a small box from his backpack. He tore open the plastic bag inside the box and fished through the sawdust to pull out a small white pod of tissue paper. As Miguel got within a few feet, José tossed the pod at Miguel's feet. Miguel was startled by the loud crack.

"What the hell are you doing?" Miguel asked.

José threw a few more. Crack! Crack!

Miguel finally figured out what was going on.

"Bang snaps? You are throwing kids' firecrackers at me?"

José grinned and held out a handful for Miguel. Miguel grabbed a few and threw them at José. Crack! Crack! After a few second of silliness, José led Miguel over to a small table and peeled open the bang snaps.

"The principle behind these bang snaps is very simple. A very tiny charge of silver fulminate makes a tiny explosion. Like a cap gun," José explained.

"So how do these fit into our plan?" Miguel asked.

"Here, let me show you." José reached into his bag and removed a regular 100-Watt incandescent light bulb from his bag and showed it to Miguel.

"I'm confused. A light bulb?" Miguel asked.

"Patience, my friend. Now, take this bulb and screw it into that light socket over there." José directed. He pointed to a shop utility lamp hooked onto the wall connected by a long extension cord. "Make sure it's off first." Miguel walked over and replaced the bulb in the light with the bulb José had just given him.

"Now hold the light out over this trash can and turn it on."

Miguel flipped the switch on the light. The sound that came next was quite interesting. If you weren't paying close attention, it sounded mostly like a regular light bulb burning out with a pop, like when you walked into a dark room, turned a switch and saw the final flash of light from the incandescent bulb before the filament fried and snapped. The pop coincided with a slightly audible breaking of glass, which was what made the sound a bit unusual and just slightly louder. Miguel actually had to turn the light fixture up to examine it. Sure enough, the top of the bulb had cracked and a piece of the bulb had fallen into the garbage can. A jagged edge of glass remained attached to the metal socket screw.

"So how did you do that?" Miguel asked.

José held up a small strip of wire with a tiny glass bubble the size of a teardrop at one end. "This wire uses the same principle of the bang snap I just threw at you. A small charge of explosive is in the bubble. We attach the wire to the base of the bulb and then adhere the bubble to the side of the bulb. When you screw in the light bulb, the wire gets hot by carrying current and then causes the bubble to burst and cracks the glass of the bulb. José demonstrated the procedure again with a different bulb, then held up the bulb for Miguel to examine.

"From arm's length, you can't even see the wire. Even if you see the glass bubble, it looks like a dollop of extra glass," Miguel observed.

"Exactly. The average consumer is never going to notice. They are going to be in such a hurry to install the bulb that they will just remove it from the package and screw it in. Then as soon as they turn it on to check the light, pop! The bulb cracks and they have a huge mess on their hands."

"I still don't get it. What is the point of blowing up light bulbs?" Miguel asked.

CHAPTER 3

Indian Ocean, off the Somali coast

"Captain, I think you'll want to see this right away. We have a distress call coming in from one of the merchant ships to the north." The young petty officer looked up from his console.

"Alright, what do we have?" Captain Tom Jackson asked as he walked over to the radar screen on the bridge of the Arleigh Burke-class destroyer.

Petty officer second class Mark Davis pointed to a small blip on the screen north of their position. "The merchant vessel Saint Marie is reporting a couple of fast boats running alongside her. Looks like they are scouting out an attack."

"Any intel on the boat crews or weapons?" Tom wanted to know what they were dealing with.

Usually these boats had a handful of young Somali men armed with AK-47s and rocket-propelled grenades, or RPGs.

"They didn't say and we are not close enough to tell at this point."

"Damn pirates, when will they ever learn?" Tom thought out loud before issuing the order. "Let's set a new course and get the helo up to check it out."

Tom thought of his fellow Americans back home, blissfully unaware of what was about to occur, even though it was all in a day's work for Tom. When most people think of the Navy, they think Top Gun and SEALs and Tomahawk missiles – all the glamor and glitz. They are often completely unaware of how much effort and dedication goes into one of the US Navy's core missions – protecting the freedom of sea lanes. Pretty much all of world commerce depends on the US Navy playing this role, and Tom Jackson went about this business seriously. He hated pirates. They were disgusting pigs.

Tom picked up the handset for the 1-MC, the ship's intercom. "Good morning, this is the captain. We are heading up north to check out some suspicious activity. Get ready. You all are professionals and this is what we train for. It's time to bring home the bacon."

A loud "sooooeeee!" erupted throughout the ship as the crew scurried to their stations. The crew had modified the "hooyah" battle cry of the SEALs into a hog call to reinforce their mission: Bringing home the bacon. The crew hated the pirate pigs as much as Tom and reveled in the opportunity to take out the bad guys.

Within the next thirty minutes the anti-piracy task force vessels converged on the scene. The helicopters arrived first. The helos were a show of force to let the pirates know that the US Navy was nearby, to gather intelligence, and deter the attack long enough to get the ships closer in.

Yet the pirates were becoming more brazen and would like nothing more than to shoot one down with an RPG and create a Black Hawk Down incident in the middle of the ocean. The main downside for the pirates is the lack of television cameras to film it – but they would try to get footage with their own handheld cameras. It was a dangerous dance for the helicopters. They needed to get close enough to divert the pirates from the merchant vessel and simultaneously stay out of range of the RPGs.

Tom Jackson had adapted to these pirates tactics by inventing laser targeting at sea. During the past two decades in Iraq and Afghanistan, US Special Forces became adept at infiltrating behind enemy lines and painting a target with a laser. Once the target was painted, laser guided missiles launched by aircraft or ship could home in on the target. Tom had innovated and adapted this approach to pirate interdiction while staying inside the confines of the politics. It was a difficult dance and sometimes Tom's aggressive approach put him on the wrong side of the political winds.

"We are on station over the St. Marie. Confirm two fast boats in a circular pattern closing in on the vessel. No signs of RPGs. Crew count unconfirmed." The radio report came in from the helo.

"Initiate laser targeting," Tom commanded. "We are closing in fast and will be in visible range in five minutes. Let's see if we can lure one of the boats to give chase."

"Roger," the helo pilot confirmed. The helicopters reduced altitude and came in behind the fast boats. Loudspeakers were blaring commands for the boats to divert from the vessel, but these announcements were mere formalities at this point. The game was on.

Tom waited as the helo pilots initiated the riskiest part of this tactical approach, The helicopters had to get low enough to lure the pirate skiffs to chase them, but that also put them potentially in range of RPGs and even machine gun fire. The helo had to stay at risk long enough to draw the pirates away from the merchant vessel and then it could climb to a safer altitude.

"Looks like one of them is taking the bait. We are initiating laser tracking."

"Roger. Waiting for your ready signal," Tom replied and turned to the fire control officer. "Make ready to fire on my command."

"Aye, sir. Weapons systems ready."

While the helicopter pilot handled the difficult maneuvering of being bait, the flight weapons officer had the more challenging task of keeping a laser on target in a radius around the fast moving boat. It would have been simpler to lock on to the target with radar and simply blow it out of the water. But thanks to the rules of engagement imposed by the international community, such measures were frowned upon, to say the least. The intent here was not to destroy the boat, but to cause the crew to surrender. This technique was the modern equivalent of the warning shot across the bow.

Once the helicopter had lured the skiff out of range and the fire command was given, the laser would guide a small missile fired from the destroyer to the surface of the water within ten meters of the pirate craft. The missile would be set to detonate a few meters below the surface, similar to a depth charge fired at enemy submarines. The resulting blast would generally cause the skiff driver to slow dramatically and surrender.

"Captain, we have a target solution."

The executive officer looked at Tom as he acknowledged the report. Tom walked to the side of the bridge where the XO whispered to him. "Permission to speak freely, sir?" Tom nodded. "Tom, are you sure you want to do this? Another week and you are home free – we'll be cruising back home through the Mediterranean. I don't want to see you get embroiled in an international incident."

"Thanks for your concern, Terry. But we've got a job to do." Tom knew that this tactic, while innovative, was pushing the envelope. So far it had worked well, but anything could happen. Tom walked back to the bridge and gave the order.

"Fire control officer, fire when ready."

"Aye, sir."

In the few seconds it would take for the missile to cover the space between the destroyer and the skiff, the second pirate boat raced into the gap and came alongside the first. Two young Somali men with RPGs on their shoulders were on the deck. One of them fired at the helo and a trail of smoke burned through the air. It was probably a waste of ammunition at that range, but he wanted to scare off the Americans. Sure enough, the errant RPG shot was enough to cause the helicopter pilot to take diversionary measures – and enough to make the laser targeting unstable.

The laser-guided shot was lucky, in the sense that the missile landed in between the two pirate skiffs – the stone hitting two birds at once. But unlucky in that instead of causing the pirates to surrender, the blast took out the back of one skiff and caused the second to capsize. Now instead of a simple surrender, Tom had a rescue mission on his hands as well. It was a pain in the ass to fish people out of the water in the open ocean. Not only that, Tom realized that maybe he had a political hot potato on his hands as well. He needed the rescue operation to happen quickly to rescue and detain all of the pirates.

Within thirty minutes, thirteen Somali men had been fished out of the water and were now assembled on the deck of the destroyer. Tom walked down to the deck to assess his prisoners and was soon face to face with the pirate leader, who was flashing his jewelry and trying to maintain his swagger.

One of the younger men in the back was breaking down and started screaming at Tom. "You bastard. You killed my brother."

"I'm sorry for your loss. Our warning shot cut it a little too close when you shot at us and your second boat moved in," Tom replied. "But if it were up to me, you'd be dead, too. All of you would be at the bottom of the ocean or hanging from the mast, for all I care. Lucky for you, it's not up to me."

The pirate leader looked Tom up and down. "Why you wanna work for the American Navy, coming back to your own continent to bust your own people?"

Tom laughed at him in pity. "You are a thief, stealing what is not yours. Pirate scum. You are not "my people." Tom walked off in disgust as the pirates were escorted to the ship's brig. Soon they would be someone else's problem.

CHAPTER 4

Mexico, south of the Arizona border.

Miguel and José arrived back at the house at dusk, just in time to complete their evening prayer ritual. When they were done and had secured their mats, José pulled two bottles of Dos Equis from the refrigerator and offered one to Miguel.

"Muchas gracias," Miguel smiled and accepted the beer. They clinked bottles and each took a long swig. Maintaining cover did have its advantages.

"De nada. Ok, are you ready?" José pulled a small USB flash drive from his pocket. "You have a computer here that is not connected to the Internet in any way, correct?"

Miguel nodded and pulled a laptop from a desk drawer. He fired it up and inserted the flash drive into one of the USB ports. After a few clicks and a password entered by José, a video player launched.

The face of Ayman Al-Zawahiri filled the screen. Nothing in the background gave any clue as to his location. A short, simple message: "My brothers, the time has come to implement a new phase in our strategy to defeat and destroy America. José, who served us valiantly in Iraq and Afghanistan and caused many deaths of infidels, will guide you to deploy our new secret weapon. Glory awaits you in paradise. Praise be to Allah."

José removed the flash drive, crushed it under his boot and threw it into the fireplace. Miguel watched him nervously. "So what is this plan for us to get to paradise? And what does it have to do with light bulbs?"

"Ha. Relax, my brother. This is not a suicide mission. There is some risk, but it will take a long time for us to get to paradise. More time for us to enjoy the virgins here on earth." José grinned and cracked open another beer for each of them.

José retrieved his small suitcase, unzipped it, and removed a small package. He tore it open and removed a white, spiral glass object and held it up for Miguel, who looked on with confusion.

"This, my friend, is a compact fluorescent light bulb, otherwise known as a CFL," José explained. José grabbed a towel from the kitchen and walked over to the lamp in the corner. He turned it off and held the towel as he unscrewed the hot incandescent bulb. He then screwed in the compact fluorescent bulb. "Ready? Watch this." Miguel nodded.

José turned on the switch to the lamp and for a second or two, nothing happened. Then the bulb flickered a few times and a dull glow filled the room. He watched Miguel's reaction, which at this point was one of complete puzzlement.

"What do you think? These bulbs last much longer than regular bulbs and use a lot less energy. Much better, right?"

"Um. Ok. But they take a few seconds to activate and the light is a bit strange," Miguel observed.

"Surely that is only a minor inconvenience for such savings, Miguel. If you install them throughout your house, think of the savings in your electricity bill."

"Maybe, I guess. So how much do they cost?"

"Well, they are a bit more expensive. About $4 per bulb, compared to traditional incandescent bulbs which are less than a dollar."

"Seriously?"

"A small price to pay to protect the environment, wouldn't you agree?"

Miguel rose from his chair and walked over to examine the CFL in the lamp.

"Be careful," José said.

"Why, is it hot?"

"Oh no, not really. I just want to make sure you don't break it. Makes quite a nasty mess."

"How so?" Miguel asked.

"Turns out that these so-called environmentally-friendly bulbs contain mercury. If they break, the entire area is contaminated. It's a real bitch to clean up – we have to secure the area, shut down the air conditioning ventilation, and try to dispose of all the dust and glass. And God help you if you happen to inhale the stuff."

Miguel walked back towards the table. "So let me get this straight. You want me to put these compact fluorescent bulbs in my house. They are four times as expensive, they don't come on right away, the light quality is weird, and if they break, I need to call in a HazMat crew? You're crazy."

"Now, now, Miguel. For a stupid terrorist, you are thinking a bit too much. Plus you don't really have a choice in the matter."

"What do you mean, I don't have a choice?"

"Not if you are in America, at least. The Americans, in their infinite wisdom, passed a law in 2007 that banned the traditional incandescent light bulb starting in 2012. The crazy cowboy George W. Bush actually signed the ban as part of the *Energy Independence and Security Act*. By the way, don't you just love how the Americans name their legislation?" José snickered.

"Why would they do that?"

"Who knows, exactly? My take is that it's a rather ingenious marriage between the environmentalists, big companies, and politicians. The environmentalists co-opt the national security message on energy independence and then get big corporations to back them. Imagine you are General Electric and you've been selling light bulbs for a hundred years at under a dollar. Along comes a new light bulb you can sell for four times as much – and you can outlaw the old one. Now every light bulb in every house and office in America needs to get replaced. The politicians all talk about green jobs, the crony CEOs get a brand new huge market, and the environmentalists slowly create their own version of Sharia law."

"Sharia? How do you figure?" Miguel asked.

"Of course you know our vision for establishing an Islamic caliphate and imposing Sharia across the world. The beauty of Sharia is that the law becomes whatever the Imam happens to say it is at any point in time. Makes things very convenient for us. The environmentalist progressives have figured out the same thing. Just write the law so it gives total discretion to bureaucrats and let your lobbyists manipulate them to do your bidding," José explained.

"I'm surprised the Americans are standing for this," Miguel said.

"Well, there has been an effort to repeal the ban, but it is going nowhere. People are asking the same questions that you did – about cost, quality, mercury risk. Some free market types are saying that the ban is a fundamental assault on freedom and liberty. But as soon as they invoke that argument, the progressive media dismisses them as a bunch of Tea Party fringe whackos. The news cycle moves on and nothing happens. The Americans get sucked into the next story about some drunk celebrity and forget about it."

"Crazy. So what does that have to do with our plan?"

"Well, imagine what happens if these bulbs start randomly breaking all over the place – homes, offices, anywhere – and spreading this mercury dust?"

"You'd probably get a lot of complaints," Miguel figured.

"To say the least. There would class action lawsuits, a 24 by 7 news media frenzy, maybe even Congressional hearings."

"So this mercury stuff. Does it really cause harm?"

"Who knows? Each side has their scientists and they all say different things."

"Who is right? What is the truth?"

José laughed heartily. "Miguel, who is to say what is the truth? Besides, that is really not our concern. We are simply going to exploit their fears. And while they are distracted with this entire mess, we create opportunities for ourselves for bigger attacks in the future."

Miguel thought for a moment and then responded. "Somehow I imagined that when it was my time we would be initiating a grand attack. Chemical or bio weapons, a dirty bomb, maybe even a nuke. You know, what do the Americans call it? A WMD – weapon of mass destruction?"

"Yes, still possible someday, but the Americans have made it very difficult. They have really restricted our ability to move people and money. We have been dealt a heavy blow with the loss of our leader, Osama Bin Laden. Their predator drone strikes are killing our brothers almost daily. Yet we must adapt our methods and tactics to continue the fight – to exploit their weakness. So now we have created a WMC."

"WMC?"

José grinned, "Weapon of Mass Chaos."

Miguel's face lit up as he realized the ingenuity of José's plan. "No wonder you've had me purchase all of these fireworks and glass blowing equipment," Miguel said.

"Yes, we are going to extract the gun powder and turn CFLs into little tiny IEDs, and then let the American consumer suffer the consequences," José explained.

"So can they trace us?"

"Maybe, but we'll be long gone by then. The amount of explosive is so tiny it vanishes in with the glass dust. It would take some serious forensics to figure it out. Most people will think it's just a manufacturing defect."

José continued, "But just to throw them off our explosives, we'll take some CFLs and make small etchings into the sides of them. This will make the glass fragile enough that they are likely to break on installation. A little too much pressure from the human hand – and snap! Same result. A big mess."

"How many bulbs are we talking about?"

"We figured a cargo container full. Probably means 50,000 or more light bulbs. Then we spread them around the United States. It will seem pretty randomized, but when enough of these bulbs start breaking in meaningful numbers, it will be enough to cause a shit storm."

"So where do we get this cargo container full of CFLs? And how do we get the bulbs into the US?" Miguel asked.

"Simple. We steal it. Well, not us, exactly. We cut a deal with some of our hermanos Mexicanos in the cartel. Our Mexican brothers will get the container for us and later help us move the bulbs across the border. I brought something for them that they would find very valuable in order to help us out."

"What's that?"

"This." José said, pulling a large brick-sized block from his bag, sealed in a plastic bag. "The finest heroin straight from the highlands of Afghanistan."

CHAPTER 5

Mediterranean Sea

"So how does it feel to be a short-timer, Captain?" Chief Petty Officer Burgess asked as he handed Tom Jackson a steaming mug of coffee.

"Right now, I'm just looking forward to better coffee. Thanks, Chief," Tom replied, causing the Chief to chuckle. Jokes about bad coffee were as old as the Navy itself. From the bridge of the Arleigh-Burke class destroyer, Tom took a sip of his coffee and scanned the horizon. The morning sun reflected off the calm waters of the Mediterranean Sea.

Tom Jackson's naval career was quickly coming to an end. The destroyer was heading back home after a six-month cruise for a change of command. According to the finest traditions of the United

States Navy, Tom would have a nice retirement party, ride off into the sunset, and collect a nice pension for the rest of his life. Maybe he'd pick up some consulting gigs here and there. And at least the coffee would definitely be better.

Actually, Tom Jackson was beginning to have second thoughts. As he looked out over the water, Tom contemplated his life – past, present, and future. Captain Thomas Jefferson Jackson, US Navy, Retired. All of it sounded great, except the retired part. Forty-three years old and retired? What was he going to do with himself?

"Well, skipper, you've had a great run here and the crew is definitely going to miss you."

"I sure appreciate that, Chief. We'll have a great party for the crew when we get home." Tom was touched by the Chief's statement, which showed the most emotion he'd ever seen coming out of the burly sailor.

"Any regrets? You still have a few weeks to find a new command. Maybe something will open up." The Chief sensed an opening to speak freely with the Commanding Officer.

"No, I'm definitely done. My only other option is

to ride a desk at the Pentagon and I have no desire to spend my days playing political games. I only wish my father could see me now."

The chief nodded knowingly as he'd lost his father at a young age. The two men returned to their coffees and stared out at the sea in silence.

As a kid, Tom spent most of his summer days and all of his weekends out on his dad's shrimp boat. Any moment he wasn't in school, he was on that boat. His dad worked the low country coastline off South Carolina, bringing his catch in each day and selling it on the docks. They never had much money, but that wasn't the point. For a black man in South Carolina, owning the boat was the dream realized. Some days were good, some were bad, but they were all his. He owned it all. Tom never heard his dad complain. In fact, just the opposite. Tom's dad reinforced the ownership mindset at every chance he could. Too many victims in the world, he said, blaming other people for their circumstance. Don't be one of them.

Tom seemed destined for the Navy from an early age. He couldn't really explain why, but his heart would sing whenever he'd get a glimpse of a naval vessel heading out of the Charleston Navy base, passing by Fort Sumter at the mouth of Charleston Harbor, and then heading out to sea to carry out its mission. No matter how close or far, he'd stand at attention and salute. By age 10, he could identify every type of ship in the fleet and knew all of the names by hull number.

Sometimes if they'd had an especially good haul, his dad would let Tom "play Navy" on the ride back in. Tom would run around the deck with a pair of binoculars, scanning the horizon, then calling out commands to orchestrate tactical maneuvers on imaginary targets. On long weekends, his dad would go out into deeper waters to fish while Tom lounged on the deck reading books on naval history.

Now here he was, in command of his own ship, finishing his career as commander of the anti-piracy task force off the coast of Somalia. Some days were good, some days were bad, but they were always interesting and always his. His dad would be proud.

Tom's dad had died when he was 14. There was no one to run the boat, so they sold it and Tom moved in with his uncle's family on the outskirts of Charleston. It was a rough time for Tom. Not only had he lost his father, but he lost his life at sea.

To fill the void, Tom got involved in sports and tried out for the high school football team. He wasn't a super athlete – other kids were bigger and faster. But Tom was smart and had great instincts to see plays develop and anticipate where the ball was moving. He quickly became a star linebacker and team captain. Other players looked to Tom as a leader. When he was recruited to play college ball and had a choice of schools, he surprised everyone by choosing Georgia Tech and also enrolling in the Navy ROTC. By his sophomore year he had established himself as a key player, but knew he would not have a future in football beyond college, Tom was simply too small for the NFL. He committed to his studies and completed his degree with a double major in mechanical engineering and economics. He graduated, pinned on his ensign's bars and was soon out in the fleet. Back at home at sea.

After his first ten years in the fleet, Tom was assigned to run part of the Naval Training Center in Chicago. Not the same as being at sea, but he liked the opportunity to train young sailors. Taking advantage of his location, Tom completed an MBA at the University of Chicago, where he made some great friends and also met Denise. She was a marketing executive on the fast track at a big consumer products company. Tom and Denise found instant chemistry and their relationship blossomed quickly. While she knew the challenges of marrying a naval officer, she agreed and they were married just after graduation.

They managed their marriage pretty well for the first couple of years. Denise worked a lot and travelled throughout the world to meet up at port calls. But then their plans diverged. Tom was promoted to Captain and offered his own ship to command. Denise urgently wanted to start a family and wanted Tom to get out of the Navy. Tom asked for a few more years, but Denise didn't want to wait and couldn't imagine raising a young child on her own with Tom at sea all the time. So she decided to leave the marriage, handing Tom divorce papers the day before he shipped out. No animosity, just a sad parting of ways.

So here he was ready to retire. But spend it doing what? And with who? All the talk of travelling the world with Denise was now a lost dream. Maybe he could stay in, he thought again. He was on the promotion list for Admiral, but that meant a staff assignment at the Pentagon. No way. Tom had no interest in dealing with all of the politics. Even though his impending civilian life was so full of unknowns, he actually was excited about the opportunity to create something new.

But enough thinking, it was time for action. Tom liked to walk the ship and greet the crew, so he refilled his coffee mug and called out to the Executive Officer to take the bridge. Tom spent the rest of the morning visiting with the crew around the ship, learning about their families and their dreams, always expressing his sincere gratitude for their service and the privilege and honor he felt to lead them. He would miss them, too.

CHAPTER 6

Washington, DC studios of Crossline

"For our final segment tonight on Crossline, we are pleased to welcome Elaine Mitchell, who joins our network tonight as a political analyst after a number of years working on Capitol Hill. Welcome, Elaine." Bob Jenkins looked into the camera and then the producers switched to a wide view to bring in Elaine sitting amongst a panel of talking heads.

"Thanks, Bob, so glad to be here."

"This week marked the implementation of the ban on incandescent light bulbs. Here's a quick look at what happened around the country," Bob said.

The video cut to a montage of footage from various incidents. The first clip showed a frenzied mob scene of consumers at a Walmart on the day before the law went into effect. A crowd of shoppers were madly stampeding in one aisle – they looked like the equivalent of a Black Friday crowd of parents shopping for the latest Elmo doll – only this time the coveted objects were 100 watt incandescent bulbs. At one point, a couple of women started fighting over the last carton of bulbs. They were playing tug of war with the package until one of the sleeves of bulbs came loose and smashed on the floor. Somehow this outcome seemed immensely satisfying to one of the women, who would rather see the bulbs destroyed. Better for them both to lose than for the other person to win.

The next few video clips showed a series of small scale protests, where a dozen people or so were gathered in the parking lots of Home Depot and Lowes stores in suburban America. A group of suburban soccer moms were focused on safety, with posters that read "No mercury in my living room. Bring back traditional bulbs." Other protestors seemed focused more on freedom, carrying the Gadsen Flag and signs that read "You'll pry my light bulbs out of my dead hands" and "Pro-Choice for Light Bulbs!"

"So Elaine, help us shed some light on what's

happening with light bulbs." Bob revelled in the chuckles from the panelists. "What do you make of all of this fuss?"

Elaine laughed and said, "Thanks, Bob. Fuss is a good word. Well, this week really is not about the protests, but about huge progress forward in terms of protecting our environment and moving towards energy independence. The fuss has already passed."

"So what about the complaints of the protestors. Some moms are complaining about the mercury. Valid concerns from moms?"

"Well, these are really nightmarish fear-mongering scenarios from uninformed people. The benefits of these compact fluorescents are quite obvious in terms of energy efficiency. The risks are quite minimal, as long as you take proper precautions. It's really important that people see the benefits of lower energy usage and the creation of green jobs," Elaine replied.

"What about the freedom argument? Should people have the freedom to choose their own light bulbs?" Bob asked.

"Oh, give me a break. Let's talk about freedom – what we want is freedom from dependence on foreign oil. Look, these right-wing tea partiers need to grow up. Moving to compact fluorescents is a quite reasonable compromise, wouldn't you say?"

"I'd sure say so, Elaine. Thanks for being with us."

"My pleasure. Thank you, Bob."

CHAPTER 7

Washington, DC.

A light rain was falling as Elaine hopped out of the cab and dashed into the lobby of the Willard Intercontinental Hotel. After checking her coat, she headed straight for the Round Robin bar. She found her contacts seated at a table in the back.

"Elaine, great job tonight." She shook hands with a man she hoped would become her first client, a senior executive at one of the largest manufacturers of compact fluorescent light bulbs. Next to him, the congressman rose from his seat and gave Elaine a big bear hug and a kiss on the cheek. "Yes, great job, Elaine. And you looked terrific."

"Thanks, gentlemen. Went pretty well, I must say." And I did look good, Elaine thought to herself.

At 33, she knew she didn't have the pristine youthful sheen of the new women who arrived in DC by the busload every year. Women seeking to bask in the power of this place. But by now, she had power of her own. Poise and seasoning. And that made for a stunningly attractive presence.

As soon as the waiter delivered Elaine's chardonnay, the congressman raised his gin & tonic to propose a toast. "Here's to you, Elaine. To your big launch." The executive echoed with "And to a bright future." The three clinked glasses and Elaine took a long, slow sip.

Today was a big day for Elaine Mitchell. She'd been working for over a year to launch her own political strategy and public relations firm. Finally she got the call and tonight was her first appearance on one of the major cable news talk shows.

Well, she wouldn't really call it news. More like political theater. But nonetheless, today was a critical step forward in her plan to reach higher levels of public service. Not naked ambition or raw lust for power, mind you, just a deep desire to serve society. That's what she told herself, at least. Now she was relishing the moment and her surroundings in one of D.C.'s power establishments.

The executive spoke first, "Really impressive performance tonight. I love how you just talk straight and tell it how it is. What's your story? How did you get to this town?"

Elaine took a small sip and began the story she'd been rehearsing. "I've always been passionate about protecting the environment for as long as I can remember. I grew up in Mill Valley, just north of the Golden Gate Bridge in San Francisco. My dad worked in the city and my mom ferried me and my sisters to all sorts of activities. Mom ran the household in between, keeping the kitchen well-stocked with fresh, organic food."

"On weekends we would take family hiking trips around the Bay Area. My parents tell a story about my first words. Apparently my dad would point at the trees and I would say "pretty" in my cutest little voice. Then they'd point to an oil refinery or a truck and I'd say "ugggly" and make a mean, scrunchy face." The executive and congressman both laughed. "My parents thought this was hilarious and wonderful. I've been on that path ever since and am thrilled to be here now, with an opportunity to serve in a bigger way." Elaine paused and took another sip of wine.

The congressman, never one to miss an opportunity to speak, jumped in. "Come on, Elaine, you're leaving out some big highlights. This girl has a degree from Yale and from the Kennedy School at Harvard in Environmental Policy. She was working a staff job at the Environmental Protection Agency when I snatched her up. I saw her testify before my subcommittee a few times and had to have her on my staff. She's been instrumental in drafting our most progressive legislation and helping me advance the cause."

"Wow, great story. Sounds like you were on the fast track. Why start your own PR firm now?" the executive asked.

The congressman jumped in, "Are you serious? Look, Elaine has the total package. Smart, brilliant, gorgeous and you can see from tonight that the TV cameras love her. She's much more valuable to us out in the media than toiling in obscurity in the back rooms of Congress."

Elaine was mildly embarrassed by the congressman, but she endured his bluster. After all, he had taken her under his wing, mentored her, and helped her set up all the contacts she would need to create her own political strategy and public relations firm. Not only would she have more influence, he told her, she could also make a lot more money. The congressman knew that his big donors also needed a media champion, or spin doctor to independently advance their agendas in the media.

Elaine knew that a few years of this gig would build name recognition, more contacts, and a nice stash of cash. Then she could run for office herself. Of course she'd need to pick up a good-looking and docile husband as a supportive political spouse, but that could certainly be arranged.

"Well, Elaine. Great to have you on board and glad to be your first client. Today was huge. We don't expect a lot of backlash from this new law going into effect, but the stakes are really high for us and we definitely want to be out in front of any news that could be problematic," The executive explained.

Elaine smiled, "Thank you, it is an honor. And of course, you have a much bigger story to tell about how your company is helping to create green jobs and energy independence."

The executive smiled at the congressman. He knew the congressman had been in this town for decades and clearly knew how to play the game. He was very pleased with the congressman's recommendation on Elaine. She knew how to play the game as well. The congressman winked back and then proposed another toast, "To Elaine Mitchell, the new face of progress."

CHAPTER 8

Naval Station Mayport, Jacksonville, Florida.

The band launched into *Anchors Aweigh* as Captain Tom Jackson saluted and walked off the dais into his retirement. Tom headed straight to the reception hall, where he would spend the next half hour shaking hands with all of the assembled VIPs and former crew. After another half hour of chit-chat, punch, cake and bad coffee, the crowd would disperse and get back to their missions. Tom usually loved the ceremony, but not when it was directed at him. He was ready for this part to be over.

After about twenty minutes of handshakes, Tom had had about enough. But then he spotted Jim Webber at the tail end of the receiving line, falling in after all of the military personnel. Jim clearly stood out in his suit and tie. Tom greeted Jim with a firm handshake, "Jim, thanks so much for coming. I didn't expect you to make it. Figured you'd be doing a deal or hobnobbing with some big investors."

Jim laughed, "Tom, there is no way I'd miss this." He and Tom had met several years ago in business school in Chicago and become good friends. Tom returned to the fleet, while Jim went on to pursue a finance career, so they'd really been out of touch for a while. "Thank you for all of your service. Congratulations on a great career and good luck in your retirement. We all depend on you and everyone here."

"Jim, I can't tell you how much I appreciate that," Tom replied.

"Let me introduce you to my business partners, Katharine and Phil. We all came down together from Connecticut. Care to join us for some golf this afternoon? We could use a fourth," Jim asked.

"Well, I was going to catch a short hop up to Charleston and go visit my uncle. But I may as well get in a round while you are here."

"Tell you what – let's play this afternoon and then I'll give you a ride back to Charleston myself. You'll like to see my new toy."

"Sounds good. Just so you know, I haven't touched a club in six months. Hard to play out in the middle of the ocean," Tom said.

"There you go, Tom, lowering expectations as usual. I'm sure that by the time we get to the back 9, you'll be in the groove."

A few hours later they were out on the course, enjoying the sun and light breeze, and catching up on old times and making small talk about kids and sports. For his first outing in several months, Tom played pretty well. As the foursome headed to the 19th hole for a beer, Tom asked Jim about his business. "Looks like you've been doing well for yourself, Jim. What have you been up to?"

"Running a hedge fund. After a few years in finance after grad school, I decided to start my own fund. Pulled together a few partners and raised a fund. We are a hedge fund in the truest sense of the word," Jim explained.

"So what do you mean by hedge fund?" Tom asked.

Jim motioned to Katharine who fielded this question. "You know the saying 'hedge your bets,' right?" Tom nodded. "Hedge fund is a popular term, but widely misunderstood. The media has latched on the term hedge fund to demonize an entire segment of the financial industry, but you really have to dig into the specific strategy of a firm to understand how it applies. The market is generally focused on conventional wisdom about how things are going to go. Hedge funds typically bet in the opposite direction in some way – trying to protect against downturns or certain scenarios."

"So how does your firm work?" Tom asked.

Phil jumped in, "Technically we are a private investment fund. We raise money from limited partners and invest it on their behalf. Some are institutional investors like pension funds and insurance companies; others are high net worth individuals. Some private investment funds are venture capital funds that invest in high tech startups; others are leveraged buyout firms that do turnarounds. We are a hedge fund, so we specifically look for opportunities to hedge risk. We are essentially betting against conventional wisdom. When the entire market thinks things are going one way, we look for ways that it might not. Then we structure our investments very creatively. Sometimes equity. Sometimes debt. Really depends on the opportunity."

The foursome gathered their clubs and hopped into a Cadillac Escalade for the short ride from the golf club out to the marina. As the vehicle pulled up a few minutes later alongside the pier, Tom's jaw dropped as he saw the glistening new racing yacht. "Looks like our ride is ready," Jim said.

"So this is the new toy you mentioned?" Tom asked. "This hedge fund gig must be going really well. What did you guys do?"

"A few years ago, during the housing boom, everyone thought that the market would keep going up. We knew it wasn't sustainable so we hedged against it. Turns out that was a really good move," Jim explained.

Jim showed Tom aboard. Katharine and Phil followed. Tom checked out the luxurious appointments and a bridge with communications equipment and electronics that rivaled the destroyer he just left. "Wow, you must have made a fortune."

A sly yet humble grin spread across Jim's face. "Yes, we did alright – and with these bad boy engines, we'll be in Charleston in no time."

That evening as they started the short cruise up the coast, Tom, Jim, Katharine, and Phil sat up on deck, eating filets and lobster tails, paired with fantastic French wines from Burgundy and Bordeaux. The sea was calm and the sky was full of stars.

"How are you doing since, um … " Jim was about to ask about Denise, but stopped as he could see he'd hit a sore point with Tom.

Tom looked out to the horizon for a moment, then back to Jim. "Hey, I'm doing alright. I understand she had to leave. Not like I'm the only sailor to ever go through that."

Katharine shifted the subject, "So, Tom, what are you going to do in your retirement?"

"Not really sure. Figured I'd head home to Charleston, fix up my house, and visit some family. Beyond that, I really don't know," Tom replied.

Jim followed up, "Pretty ironic, isn't it. You've been defending freedom for all of these years, and now you have total freedom for yourself. What do you want to create in your life?"

"That's a really great question, Jim," Tom

replied. "When you spend all of your days chasing pirates, you don't spend a lot of time thinking about it. So at least now I have time to figure it out."

"Well, if we can help, make sure to let us know," Katharine offered. Tom nodded in appreciation.

"Besides," Jim said as he refilled their wine glasses, "it not like there's any shortage of pirates out there, Tom. They are just wearing different clothes."

CHAPTER 9

Charleston, South Carolina

The morning sun glistened on the waters as Tom manned the controls of the yacht. Katharine and Jim brought up a tray of coffee and sat with Tom.

"Tom, we've been talking. We'd like to leave the yacht down here in Charleston with you for a while. Better than having her sit in the marina up in Connecticut."

"Thanks, Jim. That's very kind of you all. But I just finished command of one ship. Not sure I'm ready to deal with another."

"All of the arrangements have been made. The marina here will take care of everything. You just enjoy it," Katharine insisted.

Tom smiled and nodded, "Ok, if you insist.

Where to now?"

"The marina. We have a jet waiting to get back up to New York for a meeting this afternoon." Jim responded.

As they approached Charleston Harbor from the south, Katharine pointed to a small island at the mouth of the harbor. "What's that?" she asked.

Tom couldn't contain his surprise. "That? Fort Sumter – where the first shots of the Civil War were fired in 1861. Now it's a national monument. I've sailed past it hundreds of times."

"Oh, yes, of course. I've read about it, obviously, but never actually seen it."

"Here, I'll give you the quick tour." Tom guided the yacht on a circular arc around the historic fort. He pointed out the key features of the five-sided brick fort and described the battle that occurred there.

After the brief history lesson, Tom navigated through the harbor and into the marina. A car was waiting for Jim, Katharine, and Paul to take them to the airfield and back to New York.

Over the next few weeks, Tom pretty much

stayed on the boat and never left the marina. He took a few day trips up and down the coast, mostly cruising in and out of the Intracoastal Waterway. Between his uncle and various cousins and their friends, it was pretty easy to find a small crew of folks who'd go on day trips with him. In between the boat trips, he spent many afternoons just driving his truck around the Charleston area, playing golf, and catching up with old family friends at church picnics.

After several weeks, Tom realized that he could no longer avoid what he was dreading – returning to his house. Several years ago, he and Denise had bought a small house just after they got married. Now that she was gone, it was just an empty reminder of what might have been. Maybe he'd sell it and just live on the marina. At the very least, the house had been empty for six months and would need a good spring cleaning before putting it on the market. That would give Tom something to do.

Tom drove over to the house and started with a captain's inspection of the house. He grabbed a clipboard and worked meticulously room by room, inch by inch. In the next two hours, he identified a couple of pages worth of tasks and generated a list of supplies that he'd need to get – cleaning supplies, air conditioning filters, spackling, caulk, various nuts and bolts, and some light bulbs.

He drove out to the nearby Home Depot and quickly filled his cart with the items on his list. When he got to the last item, light bulbs, Tom wandered up and down the display for a few minutes, looking high and low. After a minute or two he stopped one of the apron-clad clerks.

"Excuse me, could you tell me where your regular light bulbs are?" Tom asked.

"Well, they are all right here. You looking for a particular type?" The clerk pointed to the display of compact fluorescent bulbs.

"No, I just need some regular light bulbs. Some 100-watts, some 60."

"Oh, you mean incandescent bulbs? We don't sell them anymore. Sorry about that."

"Do you know any place else that carries them?" Tom asked.

"Well, no, of course not. They are against the law. Everybody stopped selling them a few months ago. Is there something else I can help you with?"

Tom shook his head as the clerk walked off down the aisle, "No, thank you."

Tom pulled a package of CFLs off the rack and examined them, then put a couple in his cart. Having gathered everything on his list, he went to the check-out registers, loaded the supplies in his car, and headed home.

Within a few hours Tom had worked through many of the tasks on the list and decided to take the boat out for the afternoon. Tom cleared the marina and cruised out into the open water.

The sea was usually a source of peace for Tom, where the vastness of the water lulled him into a trance and allowed his mind to wander. But not today. Tom could not keep his mind from coming back to this question.

Light bulbs against the law? Seriously? What was that all about?

CHAPTER 10

Manzanillo, Mexico

Luis Alvarez took a seat at the truck stop counter and ordered a cup of coffee and huevos rancheros. Just as the waitress finished pouring, a fellow trucker sat next to him. "How do you think Mexico will do in the next World Cup?" he asked, motioning to the wall-mounted television showing futbol highlights. They chatted about futbol for the next few minutes as they waited for their food.

This place was a regular stop for Luis. All of his trucker buddies made fun of him for stopping so soon into a drive, but he couldn't help it. He wanted some coffee. He'd been sitting around playing cards all day, waiting for the cargo ship to unload the containers. Now he had a ten hour drive from Manzanillo to Mexico City, and he was sleepy from all of the sitting. So after driving only twenty minutes or so, Luis pulled into his favorite truck stop on the outskirts of the port town. One of his fellow drivers honked and laughed at him, racing ahead to his destination. Luis parked his truck, grabbed his big insulated mug, and went inside to fill up with coffee for the drive ahead.

As he entered the truck stop store, Luis smelled the delightful aroma of food coming from the diner area. Ah, why not have a quick bite to eat as well. He could make up the time on the road and still meet his delivery timeline to the distribution center. So he sat down at the counter and ordered huevos rancheros and coffee.

Now he was making small talk about futbol. Not his favorite sport, but it was pretty much impossible to admit that in Mexico. Besides, this guy was starting to get annoying with all his chit-chat. Luis would have preferred to sit quietly and read a newspaper.

Luis excused himself to go the restroom before his food arrived, which gave the trucker the perfect opportunity. He made sure the waitress was looking back to the kitchen, then slipped a small packet from his pocket and emptied it into Luis' coffee. Luis returned just as their food was arriving and they continued their conversation through breakfast. They paid their checks and left a tip on the counter, then got up to head back out to their trucks.

The trucker held the door open for Luis as he exited the diner. Luis tripped on the step and nearly fell.

"You ok?" asked the trucker, knowing he was not.

"Um, yeah, just didn't see that step." Luis tried to recover and continue towards his truck, but his legs were getting wobbly. "Actually, I'm going to head back in to the bathroom. Not feeling so well all of a sudden."

"Here, let me help you." The trucker put his arm around Luis's waist and turned back to the diner, leading Luis to the rest lounge near the bathrooms. The lounge had a few sofas, a large television, and a couple of arcade games in the corner. It was dark and deserted, except for the glow of electronic light coming from the screens. The trucker helped Luis to sit down and as soon as Luis hit the chair, he was out. The trucker removed Luis' jacket and placed it over him as a makeshift blanket. Then he pulled Luis' hat down over his eyes. Luis would sleep for at least twelve hours, then wake with a raging headache.

And his truck, stacked full of compact fluorescent light bulbs, would be gone.

CHAPTER 11

Greenwich, Connecticut

Tom took an early morning flight from Charleston to New York's LaGuardia Airport. The town car was waiting for him outside of the terminal and by ten a.m. he'd arrived at Jim's office in Greenwich, Connecticut.

Tom found himself fidgeting with his new suit as he entered the building. After so many years in uniform, his civilian wardrobe had lapsed into obsolescence so he'd gone shopping for some new threads. He looked at himself in the mirrored walls of the elevator, took a deep breath, and surrendered to his new identity. The Navy career was finished. Time for the next new thing, whatever that would be.

Just as Tom was coming to grips with his new identity, the elevator doors opened and he stepped into the lobby of the hedge fund offices. A young receptionist greeted Tom and guided him to a glass-walled conference room. A group of young financial analysts was spread around the conference room table, poring over a bunch of charts and spreadsheets. Apparently forewarned by Jim, one of the analysts called, "Attention on deck!" and the group stood as Tom entered. One of the young men nervously said "Good morning, Captain Jackson."

Tom chuckled as he appreciated the show of respect while shifting to his new civilian identity. "Thank you, at ease. Please call me Tom." Tom shook hands all around.

Jim and his partners walked in, "Hey, Tom, great to see you again so soon. You remember Katharine and Paul? I see you've met some of our new associates." Tom nodded as the young associates quickly gathered up their papers and exited the room. Tom and the partners took their seats around the conference table.

Katharine jumped in first, "Jim tells us you've been taking good care of our boat. Can't really keep away from the high seas, can you?"

Tom replied, "Once a sailor, always a sailor. Maybe I'll request burial at sea when my time comes."

"So how's retirement treating you?" Paul asked.

Tom laughed, "Well, as you can see, I've been officially 'retired' for less than six weeks. I'm not the kind of guy to sit around. I wanted to take Jim up on his offer to kick around some ideas with you."

Paul nodded. "Sure, that's what we love to do."

When Tom called Jim to suggest they discuss an investment idea, Jim immediately pulled his partners together. Tom still couldn't figure out why they took the meeting so quickly. He couldn't tell whether they were genuinely interested or simply being polite.

Jim sensed Tom's uneasiness and broke the tension. "Tom, we look at hundreds of investment ideas a year. We spend most of our time just thinking about different scenarios and developing an investment thesis – our theory of how to place bets based on what the market might do. Then we drill down and develop a specific investment plan.

We try to spend at least a couple of days a week meeting with different people to get their take on things. Often the best ideas come from people with the most distance from the financial markets. By the time it gets into the markets, the opportunity is gone. So I'm not sure if we'd be able to invest in your specific idea, but at least we'll have fun kicking around some ideas."

Tom relaxed and tried to feel his way in the conversation. "So what types of ideas have you been looking at lately?"

"Mostly interest rates and commodity prices. There are so many scenarios to try to sort out," Paul offered.

"Ever bet on regulatory or legal changes?" Tom asked.

Katharine weighed in, "Well, we are looking closely at which companies will win or lose as healthcare and energy regulations kick in. Some companies are much better positioned than others."

Tom probed a bit on this one, "Sure, that makes sense. But that sounds to me like straight-up equity research. I'm talking about making a contrary bet on a regulatory issue."

"What do you mean, Tom? Just give it to us straight," said Jim.

"I'm talking about making an investment that would only pay off if there was complete repeal of a law. Kind of like investing in alcohol during Prohibition."

"Wait, you aren't talking about something criminal, here? We clearly would never do that." Katharine leaned forward with concern.

"No, of course not. So hear me out on this one. Out of the past three years, I've been at sea for two-thirds of the time. Doesn't exactly leave much time for household maintenance – or to monitor domestic politics. Last week I decided to get started on some home maintenance and renovation. So I make a list of supplies and head off to Home Depot. When I try to buy some 100 watt light bulbs, I'm told by the clerk that the incandescent light bulb has been outlawed and that I can only buy these new compact fluorescent bulbs. It seemed kind of bizarre to me," Tom paused.

Katharine jumped in, "Oh, yeah. I am really not a fan of those things – ever since I found out about the mercury. I used to be gung-ho about the energy benefits, but I don't want my kids or my dogs to accidentally break one of those." Jim and Paul nodded in acknowledgement.

Tom continued, "Exactly. I'm an engineer by training, so I always go back to the triangle of tradeoffs." Tom drew a triangle on the whiteboard and labeled the sides "Good, Fast, Cheap" and then wrote "Pick Two."

"As an engineer designing any project, you always wrestle with the tradeoffs of quality, speed, and cost. I totally get that CFLs have advantages in terms of bulb life and energy consumption, but the tradeoff is higher cost and some environmental risks upon disposal due to the mercury in the bulbs."

"So do you have some way to make them cheaper or with less mercury?" Paul asked.

"No. What really irks me about the whole thing is that even if CFLs are better in some respects, why outlaw traditional bulbs – a perfectly good product that has been on the market for decades? If the CFLs were really more competitive, consumers will choose them and the traditional bulbs will die out, just like buggy whips did when the automobile came along. But buggy whips died a natural death in the marketplace instead of being legislated out of existence. Something about the whole notion just gets under my skin," Tom explained.

Katharine responded, "As the lawyer in the group, it might be worth noting that the law doesn't outlaw traditional incandescent bulbs *per se.* The law simply implemented standards for luminosity and energy efficiency and said that any light bulb must meet those standards, otherwise the manufacturer has to pay a hefty fine of $200 per bulb. It's a nice little legislative trick, since incandescents can't meet those standards."

Jim jumped in, "The law passed by a Democratic Congress and was signed by President George W. Bush with little fanfare, with the ban, or rather efficiency standards, set to go into effect starting in 2012. And of course, the average person had no idea that such a law had passed, and by 2008, the entire country was focused on economic concerns, not energy independence. There was a small effort in the House of Representatives to repeal the ban in the summer of 2010, but the bill was quashed through procedural measures. With the country focused on the debt ceiling, any momentum to repeal the ban died out and the implementation of the new standards approached unhindered."

Tom was impressed by their knowledge of the subject. After all, you don't make money running a hedge fund without a broad knowledge of business and politics. Tom took a sip of water and got ready to make his pitch.

"Exactly. So after surfing around the web and doing some research, I came up with this completely crazy idea."

CHAPTER 12

Jim, Katharine, and Paul looked at Tom and waited as Tom pulled out a manila file folder.

"Go ahead, Tom, the crazier the better," Paul replied.

"Yes, please do, Tom. We don't get paid for following conventional wisdom. In fact the more outrageous, the better – it stretches our thinking. Then we pull it apart and see what's worth pursuing," Jim added.

"Well, I started wondering how long the public will tolerate the ban on incandescent bulbs. Sure there were some initial protests when it was implemented, but they've largely faded away. So the conventional wisdom is that the ban is for real. But what if the ban were to be repealed and choice restored to the marketplace?" Tom posed the question and paused to let it sink in.

"You're right. That is crazy. Not going to happen," Paul stated.

"Exactly. So what if it did?" Tom said.

Paul started to rebut, but Jim waved him off, "Tom, please continue."

"Look, all of the manufacturing capacity for traditional bulbs has been dismantled. All of the plants are shut down and the workers laid off. I admit that I don't know what would cause the ban to be repealed, but if it were to happen, who would supply the bulbs to fulfill the pent-up demand?"

"Wouldn't the big guys just reenter the market?" Katharine asked.

"Possibly, in fact probably. But it would take them some time. These are big public companies driven by quarterly pressures from Wall Street. They have completely disposed of not only the physical assets to make traditional bulbs but they also have lost the know-how."

"Say more," Katharine nodded.

"Well, it's kind of like our golf outing after my

retirement ceremony. I really struggled on the front nine. But by the time we hit the back nine, I was getting into a groove. Know-how is like that. The big companies could re-tool, but it would take them awhile to get their people back up to speed and producing bulbs in high volumes with high quality. Plus, everything in their organizational systems is designed to slow things down."

"Ok, so what do you see as the opportunity?" Jim asked.

"Well, how about a contrarian bet on the light bulb ban. It will require some long-term patient capital. Simply put, we create a company to manufacture incandescent bulbs. We buy up the tooling equipment on the cheap, since it is all gathering dust right now anyway. There is a ton of empty industrial space around Charleston right now. Even though the federal National Labor Relations Board (NLRB) dropped their action against Boeing, the delay put a huge damper on the local economy. I think we could find a facility pretty quickly and pretty cheap."

"Ok so then what?" Paul asked.

"Well, we hire some people and start making

bulbs. We maintain a skilled labor force who knows how to make them. We stockpile the bulbs in a warehouse. If and when the bulb ban is repealed, we are the only company with a supply of bulbs and the ability to make them."

"Interesting, considering my mother-in-law has a stockpile of her own in her basement. So what's the payback?" Katharine said.

"Well, for a period of time after the ban is repealed, we are the only supplier on the market. I hate to use the "m" word, but we will be in a position to charge whatever the market will bear."

"Hey, nothing wrong with a monopoly in my book, as long as it isn't dictated by the government," Paul offered, giving voice to the "m" word.

"Well, I fully expect that other companies would come back into the market very quickly and drive the bulb prices back down to a competitive level. But my guess is that they would rather buy our company outright rather than try to rebuild it from scratch. Faster and easier that way. In any case, we have a six month to a year head start at a time when we are the only game in town," Tom replied.

"How do you keep this kind of thing secret?"

Katharine asked. "It's not exactly easy to hide a manufacturing operation with supply trucks coming in and out all day long. Plus if you start hiring, the word will get out locally. People will wonder what you are up to."

"Yes, I've thought about that. There are a number of ways to play it, but the one I'm leaning towards is to hide in plain sight. We create a company that ostensibly makes something else for the electrical industry – that would explain our investments in glass and electrical supplies and equipment. Then we have a smaller skunk-works group of employees who work on our top secret light bulb project. I figure I can hire a bunch of ex-military folks who can maintain operational security. If my analysis is correct, we can make enough money in the cover business to stay basically cash-flow neutral. I've done some preliminary models if you want to go through them," Tom offered.

"Sure, we'll definitely do that. For now, I just see one problem with this plan." Paul suggested.

"What's that?" Tom asked.

"There is zero political momentum to overturn this ban. People are preoccupied with other things now. You could be building bulbs and stockpiling for years and it never happens. Then what?" Paul asked.

"I agree. This is crazy. Nothing like repeal is going to happen," Katharine chimed in.

Tom started to reply, but Jim weighed in. "I agree with the conventional wisdom, but what if we are wrong? We are a hedge fund. So think of the cost to maintain the facility kind of like an insurance premium, or a call option, if you prefer. There's no way around it. It costs money to maintain the capability. We bet in the opposite direction all the time. Besides, we have plenty of idle cash. We could at least put it to work."

Tom waited silently and tried to read the faces of Paul and Katharine. After a few moments, Katharine broke the silence, "Ok, I'm with you, but there is still one other huge problem."

"What's that?" Jim asked.

"We're financiers, not operators. We've been betting on interest rates, commodities, and CDOs – collateralized debt obligations and swaps. We can execute that stuff since it's all paper. But for this to work, we need a leader. This idea, as far-fetched as it sounds, is completely useless without someone to run it. Someone a bit insane, if you ask me." Katharine looked at Tom. Paul and Jim nodded and gauged Tom's reaction.

"Tom, you ready for your next command? If you are on board to run this and make it work, we'll provide all of the support you need." Jim made the offer.

Tom thought for a moment. He hadn't really contemplated that side of the deal, but immediately realized the truth in Katharine's assessment. No plan was viable without a leader. And Tom was a leader. In an instant, he decided that he was all-in.

"Yes, I will do it," Tom stated with assuredness.

The three partners stood and saluted Tom, "Welcome aboard, Captain."

CHAPTER 13

Nogales Border Crossing, Mexico-US Border

"Are you sure this is going to work?" Miguel was getting fidgety as he inched their truck forward to the border checkpoint. Only about six more vehicles ahead of them and their fate would be revealed.

"Relax, amigo. Everything is good." José smiled back and nodded. He momentarily second-guessed his decision to have Miguel drive through the border, but since Miguel's Spanish and English was better, it still seemed like the better choice in case the guards were in the mood to chat.

Miguel relaxed his foot from the brake pedal and eased the truck forward again, about one full length of the vehicle, and then stopped again. He put the truck in park as each vehicle was taking a couple of minutes to be cleared through to the US. He looked over at José, whose manner was so reassuring. Thus far, José had not steered him wrong, so he saw no need to doubt him now. Yet border crossings were always unpredictable.

The momentary standstill combined with the rising heat caused Miguel's mind to wander. Everything had been quite easy up to now. Amazing what assistance a block of the finest grade Afghanistan heroin can buy. Talk about an unholy alliance – Al Qaeda and the Mexican drug cartels, teaming up to screw with the Americans.

Thanks to the cartel's assistance, the container of compact fluorescents had been easy to obtain. While Miguel had prepared their makeshift factory according to José's instructions, José left town for a couple of days to pick up the container and drive it to their secret factory.

The next several weeks had started out as sheer boredom, but they both relaxed into the work. José and Miguel were a two-man team working to sabotage an entire truckload full of CFLs. They could have done it more quickly, but that would have meant a bigger team and a compromise of security. So for weeks the two of them would wake up, conduct their morning prayers, and get to work. Carefully unpacking the bulbs, making the tiny fuses, affixing them to the bulbs, and then resealing the bulbs in their packaging. Each step was done slowly and meticulously.

Not only did the explosives need to work as designed, but the packaging needed to appear fresh. Tampered packaging would deter most customers from taking the product – they'd simply pick another one. For these bulbs to get out of the stores and into homes and offices, the packaging needed to be good. Once the bulbs were ready, they reloaded the bulbs into a smaller truck, more suitable for local or regional distribution.

Completing the entire container took about three months. After the third day, Miguel began to feel like he was in a monastery. It was tedious work, yet it somehow took on a spiritual quality. He and José worked in silence, each at their own stations, except for prayer breaks. Their only relaxation was a hike up into the surrounding hills at the end of each day.

Miguel was startled by harsh sound of barking dogs and the swift movement of border agents ahead. He looked up to see a couple of German Shepherds pulling their handlers to the back of the truck in front of them.

The border agents directed the truck in front of them out of the crossing lane and off to the side as Miguel and José looked on. The back of the truck was opened, revealing boxes of standard cargo. But the dogs persisted. Soon a false floor was discovered and five Mexicans, looking haggard and pathetic from their journey, were extracted from their hiding place. The border agents watched with satisfaction as they successfully prevented the latest batch of illegals from being smuggled through to the US.

Miguel looked nervously at José and whispered, "What happens to the people?"

"They just get sent back. No big deal. They'll try again as soon as they can scrape up the money to pay another coyote," José replied. "See, Miguel, I told you our cartel brothers would come through."

With all the excitement off to the side, the border agent gave Miguel's truck only a cursory examination. The dogs didn't detect anything – why would they? No drugs, no people. Just a truckload of compact fluorescents light bulbs.

"Documents, please?" The agent held out his hand.

Miguel handed over their passports, commercial trucking licenses and manifest. Now he'd discover if the forged documents were good enough to get them in.

"Where are you guys headed?"

"Chicago. Delivery due tomorrow morning. Driving in shifts," Miguel explained, motioning to José on his right.

The agent nodded. Tandem driving teams were not unusual for certain long haul shipments. The border agent handed back their documents and waved them through.

CHAPTER 14

Phoenix, Arizona

Three hours later, Miguel pulled into the Home Depot parking lot in Gilbert, Arizona, just outside of Phoenix. José and Miguel donned their paint-stained coveralls, faded ball caps, and work boots. They each carried a shopping bag with them and placed it into a cart as they entered the store. They walked together to the paint section and Miguel waited patiently at the counter. When the paint clerk approached, Miguel pulled a wall paper sample out of the shopping bag and explained that he wanted to match the background color. While the clerk went to work helping Miguel, José took the cart and walked down the aisle, picking up some brushes and drop cloths.

José rounded the corner and pushed the cart past

several aisles until he reached the lighting section. He picked up a few packs of CFLs and examined them. A clerk passed by and asked if he needed any assistance. No, just looking, thanks. As soon as the clerk was out of view, José pulled a package of CFLs out of his shopping bag in the cart and pretended to examine the labels closely. Over the next few minutes, he casually placed about twenty packages of tampered CFLs on the shelves, each time acting like he was comparison shopping. With his bag empty, he returned to the paint aisle. They paid cash for a couple of gallons of paint and then returned to their truck.

Mission accomplished.

Miguel and José were now ready for the next stage of their trip. They had plotted a meandering tour through the United States. They were going to take in a few baseball games, see the major sights, and quietly plant their WMCs along the way. A couple of Johnny Appleseed jihadists.

Next stop, Los Angeles.

CHAPTER 15

TJ Enterprises Factory, Charleston, South Carolina

Tom waited in the lobby of the factory, looking out the front window. The governor of South Carolina was due to arrive any minute. Tom's investment in the plant and the sudden surge in jobs had attracted the attention of several politicians, all looking for a good story on economic development.

As the governor's vehicle approached, escorted by a pair of state troopers on motorcycles, Tom walked out front to greet them.

"Welcome, Governor. Thanks for coming out to see us," Tom said to the governor.

"Well, it's not every day that someone invests this kind of money in our state and creates hundreds of jobs overnight. I wanted to meet the man behind the plan."

A few minutes of chit-chat followed as they walked into the building. Tom told his story of growing up in Charleston and his path through the Navy.

"Please tell me about your business plan for this facility," the governor asked.

Tom was not thrilled about the attention and in particular did not want to publicize the light bulb plan just yet, so he'd developed a reasonable cover story.

"We're creating a world-class R&D facility focused on fast and flexible electronics manufacturing. For years, manufacturing has been moving to China due to lower labor costs. But now their labor costs are moving up. When you include the long lead time to get cargo across the Pacific and the congestion in our major ports, the value equation starts to shift. Our thinking is that, at some point, customers will be willing to pay for critical items that they can get quickly. We can build it here and cut at least six weeks out of the process. Plus, if our relations with China ever get really dicey, we'll have a strategic manufacturing capability here at home." Tom paused, realizing he had rushed through his rehearsed spiel.

"Makes perfect sense. We've been concerned for years about the loss of manufacturing in this country," the governor replied.

"I do have one request. My investors are providing long-term capital to this idea and they know we need to keep our operations stable to build this capability. We expect to add a lot of jobs, but want to do so quietly so as to not tip off our competition. We aren't adverse to publicity, we just want to stay under the radar, so to speak," Tom said.

The governor was slightly disappointed, but understood. Better to have people off the unemployment rolls and earning money to spend, even if it meant that things needed to stay quiet. "Of course. And if you ever need any assistance, just let me know."

Chapter 16

On Facebook

Barbara Jenkins

OMG! Hank just installed a new light bulb and it shattered when it turned on!

Yesterday at 12:52pm

	Tina Smith How random! Yesterday at 12:59 pm
	Michelle Woodward Was it a CFL? Were you able to clean it up? Yesterday at 1:14pm

	Barbara Jenkins Yes. I just swept it up. Why? Yesterday at 1:32pm
	Michelle Woodward Go here and read this: http://www.epa.gov/cfl/cflcleanup.html Yesterday at 2:14pm
	Tina Smith Are you serious? What a pain in the a**! Yesterday at 2:59 pm

Barbara and Hank Jenkins were the first victims. Hank had a recliner in the living room where he'd watch sports on television and do some light reading. The incandescent bulb in the side table lamp had gone out that morning while he was reading the paper, so Barb picked up some new CFLs during her morning errands.

That evening, Hank sat down to watch some basketball when he remembered that the bulb was out. Hank shouted from the living room into the kitchen, "Hey, hon, did you pick up some light bulbs today?"

"What?" Barb turned off the sink to try to hear

him, and then realized what he was asking. "Oh, yes. They are still on the counter." She pointed to the bag.

Hank huffed and got up out of his chair to get the bulbs. He fished one of the CFLs out of the package, screwed it in to the lamp socket, and then turned the knob on the lamp.

Crack!

"Son of a bitch!" Hank screeched.

"What happened?"

"Damn bulb just broke right when I turned it on. Shattered all over my arm."

"Here go wash it off." Barb handed him a towel and sent him into the kitchen. Dust was all over his recliner and side table. She grabbed her small dustbuster vacuum and cleaned it up pretty well. She didn't think much of it until a couple of days later, when Hank developed a rash all over his forearms. The doctor said it was probably from mercury.

Over the next two weeks, this scene repeated itself hundreds of times, across Arizona and into California. A couple hundred bulbs, scattered around the major home improvement stores in a given urban area, began to find their way into homes and offices. Then the bulbs began to break as designed.

The reactions varied. Some people did nothing. Some reported the breakage to the store and tried to get replacements. Others called poison control, the Environmental Protection Agency, and even the Centers for Disease Control. Veterinarians and pediatricians were hearing about it too as people brought in their pets and children, just as precautions.

CHAPTER 17

Towson, Maryland

"Sorry to call you both out here on short notice, but we've got a bit of a situation brewing." Elaine usually met clients in a posh restaurant in DC, where the objective of these meetings was always to see and be seen, and of course to bill the lunch to somebody's fat expense account. But not this time. Now she, the congressman, and the executive were in the back corner of a hole in the wall Chinese restaurant in Towson, Maryland. No desire to be seen and no one worth being seen by.

Elaine waited for a response, but the congressman and executive offered nothing. They stayed focused on their moo shoo pork and the house special chow mein.

"I got a call this week from a former co-worker at EPA," Elaine started. "Their hotline was getting an unusual amount of call volume, all from Arizona and California, regarding shattering CFL bulbs. People were reading the clean-up instructions on the EPA website then calling to complain. Some were in a panic; many were irate."

"I say give it a few days and let it blow over," The congressman replied. The executive nodded in agreement.

Elaine turned to the executive, "Is it possible that you have a quality problem? Some kind of manufacturing defect that is causing these bulbs to break? It's just a matter of time before this kind of news could go viral."

"First of all, we aren't even sure if those bulbs are ours. We do have competitors, you know," The executive replied.

Elaine tried to read between the lines. "Look, there are no lawyers around here, as far as I can tell." She pointed around the empty restaurant. "But aren't you even looking into what's going on? Conducting an internal investigation, at least?"

"Well of course we are. I'm sure our people are

looking into it. We can't afford that kind of investigation or, heaven forbid, a recall. I just can't even suggest that on the record. Look what happened to Toyota with their runaway brake systems. It was human error but the media twisted it every which way. I agree with the congressman. Let's wait this thing out."

"But how do we know it's over? Could there be more bad bulbs? These things are made in China, right? Maybe a whole shipment went bad," Elaine pressed.

"Not ours. Our manufacturing standards are the best in the world," The executive asserted.

"Ok, so maybe the bulbs are from your competitor. But that still poses a risk to the entire industry," Elaine responded.

"And to the entire movement," The congressman added, then looked to the executive. "You know, Elaine has a point here. Wouldn't want to jeopardize all of our progress in reinventing your industry."

The executive paused for a moment and poured some more green tea. "Elaine, you are supposed to be the best in business, right? The new face on the scene? The media pundit?" His eyes penetrated into

Elaine. "Come up with something. Make it about human error. Maybe people are twisting them too hard and causing them to break."

"What do you mean, a sudden outbreak of stupidity throughout California? It wouldn't be the first time." The congressman laughed at his own joke.

"We talked about this before you got here. I agree. We've made too much progress on this front. This is only a minor setback. We just need to ride it out." The executive wiped his hands on his napkin and pushed back from the table.

The congressman stood and looked down at Elaine, "You're a smart girl, Elaine. I'm sure those fat fees you're getting from our friend here can inspire lots of creativity in you to come up with a response."

Elaine watched the two leave and hop into a town car waiting out front. She had gotten the message. Make this problem go away.

CHAPTER 18

Washington, D.C.

Elaine Mitchell was prepping her talking points for her upcoming television appearance when her cell phone vibrated.

Text message from Eric. *Need to see you ASAP. Plz come to Boston tonight.*

Eric was a good friend from graduate school. They met at a mixer while Eric was at MIT and Elaine at Harvard. He was a computer geek with halfway decent social skills, and he was cute besides. They were both intently focused on their studies, but would still get together for the occasional hook up. Friends with benefits.

Elaine texted back. *Can't today. News appearance Sunday morning. Prepping big time.*

Two seconds later her phone rang. Eric's photo appeared on the screen. She let it go through to voice mail. She had to stay focused on her talking points for tomorrow's show.

The phone buzzed again. Another text. *Elaine. Urgent. Must talk to you.*

She set her pen down and called Eric, "What's going on?"

"You need to get on the next shuttle up to Boston. I've got something you must see. It's about the CFLs that are breaking across the country."

"Can you please come down here? I'm really busy here. Plus I'll make it worth your while," Elaine suggested.

"Look, ordinarily I'd totally take you up on that, but you must come here to see what I'm talking about. I'm pulling data from several disparate systems and I can't just move my gear down there. I know how busy you are getting famous, but you've simply got to see this before someone else figures it out," Eric persisted.

"Ok, let me call the producer and see if I can do a remote appearance from Boston. Maybe this stuff you've got will give me some news to break. He'll love it," Elaine said.

"Well, I'm not sure about that. You can see for yourself. Just get her as fast as you can. You know where to find me," Eric said then disconnected.

Thirty minutes later, Elaine was in a cab heading to Reagan National. She'd paid a huge premium to get a seat on the shuttle at short notice, but she did trust Eric. Not that they'd ever talked much substance, but she had no reason to think he'd ever steer her wrong.

A few hours later she found Eric at his usual hangout, a coffee shop in the middle of Cambridge. He was working on one of his several laptops. An empty espresso cup and crumbs from some type of pastry were strewn across the table. As soon as he saw her, he swiftly packed up his gear and led Elaine out of the shop.

Without even a hug or peck on the cheek? Elaine's sense of alarm was growing. "Eric, why the rush?"

"You'll see. Come on, walk faster. I'll explain as we go." Elaine picked up her pace and regretted wearing heels, but she hadn't had time to switch shoes.

"I've been working on this new computer application to do data mining of social media. All of the Facebook posts and Twitter tweets create this massive amount of unstructured data. Me and some of the guys are trying to see if we can sift through all of it to identify patterns and create actionable intelligence out of it," Eric explained.

"Who cares?"

"Well, I hope that someday Google will care and maybe buy a company that I create, but for now, it's specifically the Department of State. The Arab Spring uprisings in Egypt and throughout the Middle East caught State totally by surprise – especially how events were catalyzed by Twitter and other web technology. Problem is, they don't have any way to monitor events fast enough and figure out what's really going on – or who the key players are. They wrote us a big check to accelerate our data mining research."

"Makes sense," Elaine nodded, struggling to keep up. "So what does this have to do with the CFLs breaking. Or more specifically, me?"

"Just a minute, and I'll explain everything." Eric

pulled out his keys as they approached the door to his computer lab. A few minutes later, they were inside his office. Several large flat screen monitors were set up around the room, and Elaine almost tripped over a bunch of cables running across the floor.

"Sorry this place is such a mess. We are rigging it up so fast that I haven't had time to neaten it up." Eric moved a pile of journals from a chair and offered it to Elaine. She sat and rolled the chair up next to him.

Eric grabbed a mouse and clicked to pull up his Facebook page. "Check this out. A post on Facebook or Twitter is like a pebble thrown into a pond. It makes a splash, and then ripples out as people comment and repost it."

Then he pointed to another screen, which at the moment was scrolling through lines of text. Elaine looked confused.

"What we've done is to create a program that looks for all the ripples on a particular topic and then traces them back to the original pebble. That part is pretty easy. You just work backward in the thread to find the original post. The hard part is looking for ripples caused by ripples and also tying these ripples to other sources of data to paint a picture of what's going on. Even though our State Department funders care mostly about the Middle East, we use all sorts of current events to try to improve our system."

"So we start with monitoring the trending topics on Twitter. That tells us what people are tweeting about the most." He pointed to a chart printed out taped to a whiteboard. "About two weeks ago, we started seeing "CFLs" and "Cleanup" and "Breaking CFLs" start showing up. Way above any normal level of traffic on those terms. Also cross-checked with Google Adwords and notice that keyword searches on those topics are going up fast. You know anything about this through your EPA buddies or folks on the Hill?"

"No, not really," Elaine tried to deflect, but Eric saw through it.

"Ok, whatever," Eric continued. "So based on this uptick in traffic about CFLs, we ran our trace algorithms on the ripples, so to speak. The key here is to cross-reference the ripples with geographic data. The challenge is that on the web, people can post from anywhere – a mobile device, a browser. But that's really our secret sauce," Eric bragged for a moment, but Elaine did not seem impressed.

"So anyway, then we took the original ripples and traced by geography. We plotted the reports of breaking bulbs on the map."

Elaine studied the Google map with pins all over the place.

"I don't get it. You've got reports of breakage in most every major and mid-tier city. Plus these random reports all over the place," Elaine said.

"Yes, that's what I thought at first. But here's where our program still needs some human tweaking. Turns out that some of the initial posts, or pebbles, were not from the actual victim, if you want to call it that, but from a friend or family member. For example, you put a bulb in, it breaks, you call a friend or relative, and that person posts it. So they are creating a ripple somewhere else, even though the event happened in a different place," Eric explained.

"So how do you get the data on where these people are?"

"That part is so easy, it's scary. Sometimes it is readily available in their own profiles. Other times we access commercial databases, credit bureaus, pharmacy prescription reporting systems, and log IP addresses."

"What does that tell you?" Elaine asked.

"Here. This is an adjusted map that corresponds to the actual locations of breakages. We had to make some human guesses and may be wrong, but we think we've removed all the noise. The map pins you see now correspond to breakages."

"Sorry, I still don't get it. Still looks like major and mid-tier cities – with some of that noise removed," Elaine responded.

"Yes, but now watch this – it's a time-stamped animation of the reports. We cross-matched the geo data with the date and time of the original posts. Think about it – as soon as the bulb breaks, someone posts about it. So now we have an animated timeline. Let me show you."

Eric clicked on the play icon to start the mapping sequence. Map pins started appearing on the map while an elapsed time bar grew from left to right along the bottom of the screen.

CHAPTER 19

Cambridge, Massachusetts

Elaine watched as the first pins appeared in Phoenix and grew into a flower-like cluster around the city. Then there would be a delay, then pin clusters would show up in another city. Phoenix. Los Angeles. San Francisco. Reno. Salt Lake City. Denver. Omaha. Minneapolis. Madison. Chicago. Indianapolis. Cleveland. Pittsburgh. Then the animation stopped.

"Bizarre. Looks like some kind of virus travelling around and infecting people. And Phoenix is our ground-zero?" Elaine asked.

"Well, a virus would have a more randomized scatter pattern starting from the initial point of infection. This is not random at all." Eric explained.

"Let's zoom in and slow down the time scale. What we found is that most of the breakages in a particular city would occur within a one week period from the initial report, and then stop. Then a few days later, breakages start in another city. I'm going to pause between each city so you can see what I'm talking about. Let's start in Phoenix. Initial reports start on Day 1 and the cluster of reports in Phoenix occur mostly within the next four days, then tail off."

"Got it," Elaine nodded.

"So now look at the first reports from Los Angeles. They occur on Day 3. About two days after the initial reports in Phoenix. Then San Francisco starts showing up on Day 5, and Reno on Day 7. Then we have a three day gap before we see reports in Salt Lake City. And so it goes. Here's a chart of the time gap between each cluster." Eric clicked to a different part of the monitor and brought up a graph.

"So what does this tell us?" Elaine asked.

"Remember that summer in grad school when we went out to California to pick up your car from your parents, and then we drove across country from California to Boston?" Eric said.

"Don't remind me. Four days of sitting on my ass. Although I did enjoy the company," Elaine smiled.

"Exactly. So remember the long stretch across the Midwest? Between Denver and Omaha."

"Twelve hours straight of prairie and corn. Sorry, Eric. What's the point?" Elaine was getting impatient.

"The time delays between these city clusters corresponds almost exactly to the drive time between cities. Figure seventy miles per hour, rest breaks, and a stop for the night."

"That means it's not a manufacturing quality problem. Somebody has sabotaged the bulbs and is hand-delivering them across the country. Who?"

"No idea. But we come to the same conclusion. If it were one large shipment that was defective, you'd see that centered around one major metro area or region. A truckload would go into a distribution center and the bulbs would get stocked in stores in that area. We'd see concentration of breakages in one area within a pretty compressed time frame.

And we'd see much larger numbers in one area. Instead, we are seeing a break here, break there. Much smaller quantities – ten or twenty reports in a city. Then wait a day or two, and similar numbers in the next city. When we drill down even further, we can make a good guess as to the specific store where the bad bulbs originated."

"So how are they getting on the shelves?"

"You ever shop at a Home Depot? Sorry, silly question." Eric knew that Elaine's well-manicured hands never touched anything as mundane as a socket wrench.

"My best guess is that someone is driving across the country, walking into a Home Depot, and simply putting these bulbs on the shelf. Then they leave. An unsuspecting customer picks them up, buys them, goes home and bam. They break. By that time our delivery person is driving to the next city. A day later, the pattern starts again."

"Who would do that? And why?"

"No idea. Not really my department."

"So if the last report is Pittsburgh, where are they headed next?"

"Again, not my department, but they could drive to anywhere on the northeast United States within a day."

"Including DC?"

"Of course. They could be there in an afternoon. Who knows, they may be there already."

"Crap." Elaine pondered her situation for a moment. "Ok, I have to run. Text me immediately as soon as you see clusters show up anywhere else."

"You aren't going to stay for the night?" Eric asked, hopefully.

Elaine gave him a quick kiss and broke away, "I promise I'll make it up to you later."

"One other thing, Eric. When you say 'we' – who else knows about this?" Elaine asked.

"Well, we is a few guys who built the overall program. No one really knows about the CFL specifics but me," Eric replied.

"Good, let's keep it that way," And with that, she headed for the door.

CHAPTER 20

Washington, D.C.

Elaine had just started to doze off on her couch when her phone buzzed. She sluggishly reached for the phone. Eric.

"Hey, Eric, what's up?" Elaine mumbled.

"Have you seen the Baby Zoe video yet?" Eric asked.

"Baby Zoe? What are you talking about?"

"Just go to YouTube and search for it. Then call me back."

After a few clicks, Elaine found a series of videos with Baby Zoe in the title, all uploaded by the same user. She clicked on the oldest one first. Soon the video started and showed a beautiful young woman who appeared to be in her late 20's. She looked pregnant, but Elaine couldn't tell how far along. The woman was singing sweetly while painting a mural on the walls of what would be a baby's room. The camera zoomed in as she put the finishing touches on a giraffe. Noah's Ark theme. Adorable, thought Elaine.

She clicked through the next few videos in the series. It looked like this couple was doing their own reality show, filming every moment of their baby's life even before it was born. First time parents, for sure.

Elaine came to the last video. The woman is walking, or actually sort of waddling through the moderately sized apartment. Camera pans down slightly as the woman rubs her belly. Probably eight months pregnant by now, Elaine figures.

"Hi Zoe!" the mom-to-be says to the camera as she rubs her belly. "Your daddy and I are so excited to meet you – just a few weeks to go and you'll be here. We've been working on your room for you and today is the big reveal!" She turned and headed down the short hallway as the camera followed. She gently pushed open the door to the nursery, which was still dark except for a glimmer of sunlight creeping through the edge of the window shades.

"Here's your crib and a wonderful rocking chair where we can sit together and read stories. Your new lamps arrived today from Pottery Barn. Are you ready to see it?" Elaine thought this was getting a little wacky. When is this kid ever going to watch this? And will it ever care about a lamp from Pottery Barn?

The mom sat down in the rocking chair and reached up to the lamp. As she turned the switch, there was a pop-pop-smash-smash sound as a couple of bulbs shattered. The mom-to-be freaked out and started screaming. Glass was everywhere. The camera wavered as the father rushed forward, not knowing in that instant whether to keep filming or to attend to his wife. He set the camera up on a dresser and came into the shot for the first time as he tried to calm his wife down. But she would have none of it and insisted on calling an ambulance.

"Are you hurt?" he asked. "What's an ambulance going to do?"

She kept screaming hysterically, "Just do something!!!"

The father went off in search of his cellphone to call EMS. Clueless about what to do next, the father-to-be went back to his camera. The camera panned out, looking around the area. Dust and glass was all over the crib, the rocking chair, and the woman's belly. The camera panned up and zoomed into the light fixture and saw the stems of the bulbs, still in their sockets with shards protruding. More hysterical screaming.

The video kept running as the EMS crew arrived. Elaine kept watching, as the mom insisted on a makeshift hazmat station. "Get this stuff off me, now!" she screamed. The EMS crew led her out of the apartment to the parking lot below, where an ambulance and fire truck were standing by. The female EMS tech quickly rigged up a privacy screen. She helped the woman step behind the screen and stripped off her clothes. Then they put a fire hose on low pressure and hosed her down. Then the camera stopped.

Elaine was about to restart the video when she looked in the lower corner. 176,483 views since being posted yesterday. She refreshed the page. 178,722 views now. She reviewed the clip again, watching the mom's hysteria. Refresh. 184,063 views.

Damn, Elaine thought. This thing was going viral.

PART II

"The preservation and expansion of freedom are today threatened from two directions. The one threat is obvious and clear. It is the external threat coming from the evil men in the Kremlin who promise to bury us. The other threat is far more subtle. It is the internal threat coming from men of good intentions and good will who wish to reform us. Impatient with the slowness of persuasion and example to achieve the great social changes they envision, they are anxious to use the power of the state to achieve their end and confident in their own ability to do so. Yet if they gained power, they would fail to achieve their immediate aims and, in addition, would produce a collective state from which they would recoil in horror and of which they would be among the first victims. Concentrated power is not rendered harmless by the good intentions of those who create it."

– *Milton Friedman*

CHAPTER 21

Bowie, Maryland

"Elaine, what the hell is going on? Don't you know there's a game today?" The congressman was clearly irked by the interruption. Elaine sensed the congressman probably had a good buzz on. She could hear a sports announcer in the background and realized he was out at FedEx Field. Ah, should have known. Redskins football was the unofficial religion in this town.

After seeing the Baby Zoe video on Sunday afternoon, Elaine debated whether to call the congressman. He had a private cell phone number for emergencies only. Was this an emergency? Elaine had so far managed to keep a lid on the CFL story. Even though some local newspapers in mid-tier cities had reported on CFL breakages, these reports were barely blips on the radar of bigger national news organizations.

Elaine was exhausted. After multiple TV appearances this past week as a political analyst, she knew from her producer that the show's ratings had gone up significantly since they had signed her. Her clients were pleased, her producer was pleased, and Elaine was pleased. She just wanted some time curled up on the couch for some well-deserved relaxation before jumping back into the fray on Monday morning.

After dozing off for a few minutes, she rechecked the Baby Zoe video. The view count was skyrocketing and Elaine was now fully awake. She decided she couldn't wait and dialed the Congressman's private number. He didn't answer at first, and she'd left three urgent messages and was pacing around her apartment when he finally called back.

"Sorry to interrupt. But we've got a big problem. Have you seen the Baby Zoe video yet?"

"No, what are you talking about?"

Elaine briefly explained, "Go lock yourself in a bathroom stall or something and watch it on your smartphone. Then get a hold of our executive sponsor. We've got to meet ASAP and figure out how to play it."

"Actually, he's here with me. Well, more like I'm here with him. How else do you think I scored these skybox tickets? Meet us for dinner out this way after the game."

They met in a small Japanese restaurant in Bowie, going east from the stadium out towards Annapolis while everyone else was headed back into the city. The executive was not happy to be diverted from his Sunday evening plans.

"Elaine, I thought you were going to take care of this little problem," he started in as they washed their hands with the hot hand towels. Not even a moment of preliminary chit-chat.

"Look, we've managed to keep it pretty quiet over the past couple of weeks. But this Baby Zoe video changes everything. We need to get out in front of this story, fast," Elaine explained.

"Alright, what do you have in mind?" the Congressman asked, trying to defuse the situation a bit.

"I have an idea, but I need to make sure we're on the same page first." Elaine had been mulling her next question over in her mind all afternoon, thinking about what Eric had showed her up in Boston, and wondering how the executive and congressman would react.

She decided to float a question first. "Any developments in your internal investigation?" Elaine asked and then took a sip of her tea.

The executive shifted uncomfortably in his seat. He pulled the wooden chopsticks out of their paper wrapper, broke them apart and rubbed them together to smooth off the rough edges. He was composing his statement carefully.

"Well, from what we can tell, all of the broken bulbs originated from one cargo container. This container was stolen in Mexico about eight months ago," He replied.

"Stolen, why?" asked the Congressman.

"Who knows? Cargo theft is a huge problem. Thieves mostly steal electronics and pharmaceuticals. Why the hell they'd steal a bunch of light bulbs is beyond me. At any rate, we reported it to our internal loss folks back when it happened. They looked into it, figured it was a random event, and wrote it off."

"No insurance claim?" Elaine asked.

"No, not in this case. We're a huge conglomerate and have a small percentage of theft losses across the entire company all the time. So we essentially self-insure. Just a cost of doing business," he shrugged.

"So are you sure they are all from this one shipment? And any idea why these bulbs are breaking?" Elaine asked.

The executive's face tightened up and then relaxed, as if he'd been rehearsing what he was about to say. "No, we don't know. The entire lot passed QC ... Quality Control ... at the factory outside Shanghai. Whether there was a slip-up there or somewhere else along the line, we don't really know."

The sushi arrived, which was a blessing to Elaine as it bought her some time. As they stuffed their faces with assorted maki, she contemplated her next move. No mention of tampering. Why would he? It was risky to press him on this one. Besides that was really just Eric's theory. Elaine didn't like it, but she had a job to do and she was going to do it.

"Ok, Elaine, you are the media expert. What's your plan." The executive asked. The Congressman peered up from the end of his chopsticks to assess Elaine's face.

Elaine hesitated for a moment.

"C'mon Elaine, spill it," the executive pressed her.

"Alright, look," she relented. "You want this to go away, right? Get sales back on track and protect this market?" The exec nodded slightly, his eyes saying I'm still listening.

Elaine looked to the congressman, "You want to look like you are doing something about this little hiccup but not compromise the bigger picture. Fair?" The congressman nodded in agreement.

"So, tomorrow morning, you call a press conference to announce investigative hearings in your sub-committee based on the Baby Zoe video. Our friend here comes in for a couple of days and you get to beat him up in front of the cameras. The company admits to a stolen container and agrees to a fine and some additional preventative security measures. Within a few days this all blows over."

"What about our civil liability? Aren't we just handing a case to the plaintiff sharks out there?" the executive asked.

"Maybe a little, but your exposure is pretty small. Sure some class action lawyer will no doubt find a lead plaintiff, form a class, and sue you, but so what. You guys have hordes of lawyers dealing with this stuff all the time and you are only talking about a handful of cases here. Your liability is tenuous at best – your bulbs passed QC at the factory, they were stolen, for Pete's sake. Once something gets stolen from you, how much liability can you really have?"

"Besides, these folks have to prove damages. Maybe you have to replace some carpeting for folks here and there, but in terms of long term health risks, how can they prove it?

The executive and congressman both grinned, "You have a great mind for this work, Elaine. You'll go a long way in this town."

As Elaine drove back into the city, she kept

wondering what that really meant.

CHAPTER 22

Dulles International Airport, Virginia

Miguel stirred the sugar into his venti cappuccino, replaced the plastic lid, and walked away from the Starbucks in search of his gate. He had a couple of hours to kill before his flight to Madrid. José had taken an earlier flight to Amsterdam out of Newark. They planned to reconvene in Paris in a few days to debrief the mission.

He walked along the concourse, sipping his coffee, wheeling his rollerboard behind him. Wearing a blue pin-striped suit, dress shirt with no tie, and a fresh shave, he looked like just another businessman waiting for an overnight flight to Europe. Miguel passed by one of the news shops and stopped at the outer edge. Passengers were roaming the store, browsing paperbacks and buying bottled water. He picked up a USA Today to read the cover story.

"CFLs Hearings Wrap Up With Focus on Quality." Below the headline, a photo showed a corporate executive testifying, with a number of representatives and staffers out of focus in the background. Miguel read on, "The hearings on CFL safety concluded Thursday after executives at the leading supplier confirmed the damaged bulbs had been isolated to one small shipment stolen in transit."

Miguel read on, noting the quote from a congressman at the close of the hearings, "The American people can rest easy tonight. The manufacturer will pay a large fine and clearly face civil liability for those harmed by this incident. We are assured that CFLs are safe. I'm personally pleased that we can put this episode behind us and can continue to move forward towards energy independence."

Miguel cocked his head and made a puzzled face, trying to figure out what the heck that meant. He paid for the paper, stuffed it into his bag and walked on down the concourse. After passing a few gates, he noticed a crowd of about twenty people straining their necks upward to watch a flat screen TV. "What's going on?" he asked a woman standing on the periphery.

"Not sure exactly. CNN is reporting some kind of incident at the Capitol," she replied.

Miguel nodded and looked up to see for himself. The reporter on screen was reporting, "The US Capitol has been evacuated and secured after a bizarre incident that occurred just moments ago on the Capitol steps. One congressman has been taken to the hospital as a precaution and hazmat crews are on the scene here."

The anchor back in Atlanta said, "Thanks Bob. We're going to show the incident footage again."

Miguel watched as the video played. The congressman whose picture he'd just seen in USA Today was walking down the Capitol steps with a small entourage of staffers. A reporter was a few steps in front of him, walking backwards down the steps while trying to interview the representative. Then, like a bizarre flash mob Miguel had seen on YouTube, a group of about 100 protestors converged around the congressman from several different directions. Now he was trapped on the Capitol steps.

The crowd was surprisingly calm, but that made the congressman even more nervous. It was one thing to be confronted by an unruly mob. But a ruly mob? They were calm and collected. The congressman decided to play it cool.

"How can I help you?" he asked.

An apparent spokesperson emerged from the crowd. "We just have one question for you, sir. Why did your hearings not even consider the possibility of repealing the ban on incandescent light bulbs?"

"Well, the hearings were clearly focused on CFL safety. We confirmed that this unfortunate incident is isolated and the manufacturer is taking responsibility. CFLs do not pose a threat to anyone's safety."

The reporter now realized he was in the middle of a great story and snapped to attention. He became the impromptu debate moderator and put the microphone back to the protestor spokesperson, "How do you respond?"

The spokesperson looked the congressman in the eye and spoke to him, not the camera, "Congressman, I accept your assertion that the bulbs are 'safe'. If you would like to put those bulbs in your house, that's your choice. What I would like to know is, why do you continue to deny that choice to us? Why can't we decide for ourselves whether we want CFLs or incandescents in our homes?"

The reporter shifted the mic back to the Congressman, who replied, "Sir, CFLs are a major leap forward in energy efficiency and environmental protection. They are vital for the energy independence of the United States. You look like a smart man, surely you can see that. Now, if you'll excuse me, I have an appointment to get to."

Rather than close in to detain him, the crowd actually opened up and offered him clear passage. The Congressman began to move down the steps.

What happened next would become known as "the mercury Molotov cocktail," and since the camera was tracking the Congressman, the perpetrator would never be identified. Somewhere from within the crowd a voice shouted, "Hey, Congressman. One more thing…." As the congressman turned to look back, the voice continued "Here, if you want CFLs in your house, take them!"

At this point the congressman tried to dodge and duck, but it was too late. A cluster of about a dozen CFL bulbs were lobbed from somewhere in the crowd and landed right at his feet. The crowd rapidly dispersed to various points on the mall as the congressman found himself standing in a puddle of glass shards and mercury dust. The camera zoomed out as the cameraman stepped back to get away from the hazard. The clip ended and the anchor resumed his speculative banter with the on-scene reporter.

In the airport, Miguel watched for a few more minutes, but they essentially repeated the same story over and over. He left and headed to his gate, wondering how the bystanders could stand to watch this repetitive chatter.

A few minutes later he was on board the Airbus 330, reclining in his business class seat and reflecting on his journey with José that began months ago. Forget WMDs, he said. We will create WMCs. Weapons of Mass Chaos.

The flight attendant brought him a gin and tonic. He took a sip, swirled and crunched on some ice, and peered out the window as the plane pushed back from the gate. As the Airbus lifted off, he thought about the crazy scene in front of the Capitol and smiled to himself. Chaos. Mission accomplished.

CHAPTER 23

TJ Enterprises Factory, Charleston, South Carolina

Tom was pacing around his office, watching the factory activity through the glass windows while keeping one eye on the flat screen monitors surrounding his desk. The phone rang and Tom noted the caller ID for his friend and now main investor. "Good morning, Jim. What's going on?"

"You watching these hearings?" Jim asked.

"Unfortunately, yes. Like watching paint dry. I've got C-SPAN on one screen and I'm monitoring all the news chatter on the other." Tom glanced up at the displays that surrounded his desk.

"Looks optimistic. We could be in business much sooner than we thought. Man, after the Baby Zoe video and the Molotov cocktail incident at the

Capitol, the calls for repealing the bulb ban have been deafening. I hear the switchboards in DC have been overwhelmed with calls for repeal," Jim said.

"Maybe, I'm trying not to get my hopes up too much." Tom tried to diffuse Jim's salivating optimism with a dose of realism. "Quick, Jim, turn on Crossline – looks like they are about to talk about this." Tom turned up the volume and focused on the screen.

"Welcome back, Elaine. What's the latest status of this repeal bill?" Bob Jenkins shuffled some papers as he transitioned to the next segment of the show.

"Well, Bob. Even though there is some public pressure, a complete repeal is extremely short-sighted. Imagine if we were to dismantle all of our progress on environmental protection, energy independence, and green jobs just because of a temporary manufacturing glitch," Elaine explained.

"Absolutely, yet it looks like we are at a standstill with two competing bills on this issue. Can you explain the difference?" Bob asked.

"Well of course one side wants a complete and permanent repeal, to be implemented immediately.

As I just said, this approach would dismantle everything. As the subcommittee chairman is advocating, the much more reasonable alternative is to offer temporary one year repeal and to delay its implementation for a year to make sure that quality standards can be met," Elaine explained.

Tom checked to see if Jim was still on the line. "Do you hear that, Jim? What the hell is that about?"

"Just follow the money. A temporary repeal would preserve the long-term market for CFLs. A one year delay would give the same suppliers some time to tool up to sell incandescents during that one year repeal," Jim figured.

"Can you believe these people?" Tom ranted. "The very congressman who was on the receiving end of the thrown bulbs is now gumming up the repeal process. You think he'd just let it go, but he insists on extracting some kind of concessions. Sheer lunacy."

"Just business as usual," Jim replied.

Tom turned back to the monitors.

"Elaine, I'm getting word that a new proposal is coming to the floor. We're going to cover it live, standby," Bob Jenkins announced.

The congressman rapped his gavel and spoke, "Ladies and gentlemen, I'd like to propose a compromise – a one-year waiver, to be implemented immediately."

"Woo-hoo!" Jim cheered through the phone.

Tom tried to stay focused on the screen.

"Elaine, this looks like a breakthrough. What do you make of it?" Bob asked.

"The congressman looks like King Solomon splitting the baby. What a display of bipartisanship. This gives manufacturers time to ensure the safety of the CFL manufacturing process and makes sure we don't lose the huge gains we are making in energy independence and green jobs. Brilliant!" Elaine exuded enthusiasm in her comments.

Tom had seen enough. "Well, I still don't know what to make of these people, but it looks like at least we're officially in business – for a year, at least."

CHAPTER 24

TJ Enterprises Factory, Charleston, South Carolina

"All right everyone, gather around. First auction goes live in thirty seconds," Tom smiled at the feeling of being in command, like he was giving the firing order from the bridge.

A big cheer erupted from all of the associates, and then the factory floor fell silent in anticipation as they gathered around the trading desk in the operations center. Just like the combat information center aboard his destroyer or a Wall Street trading floor, this room was designed to be the true center of intelligence and power for the company. Flat panel screens covered every available surface. Major news outlets like CNN, Fox, MSNBC, and CNBC were on one set of screens. Another screen showed real-time manufacturing status. A huge map showed shipping status of trucks as they moved across the country. And right in the center of it all, a crew of sales specialists and analysts manned the auction workstation.

"Alright, here we go. 3, 2, 1. We are live," the sales specialist announced.

Nothing happened at first. A few seconds went by, and then the first bid came in just above the minimum bid of $1 per bulb. As the clock counted down, the activity started to pick up. Bids came in at $1.25, then $1.50, then $1.75.

"Thirty seconds remaining," the specialist announced, even though the clock was displayed for all to see.

Tick. Tick. Tick.

All of a sudden a huge jump. $3.00. Then a flurry of final bids. $3.50. $3.75. Then as the final ticks of the clock counted off, $4.25.

"SOLD at $4.25," the specialist announced, but he was barely audible amidst the cheers that erupted from the room.

CHAPTER 25

TJ Enterprises Factory, Charleston, South Carolina

Tom couldn't quite put a finger on it, but he was still uneasy. Maybe it was just the captain's mindset that he'd developed through his career. Even when things were going well, something could and often did go wrong. So he was always on the lookout.

Jim, Katharine, and Paul, on the other hand, could not contain their excitement. They had flown down to check on their prized investment, TJ Enterprises, and then take in a couple of rounds of golf out on Kiawah Island. Once again, they looked like geniuses for making this investment. Not only did they stand to make a huge pile of cash out of this deal, they were the talk of the hedge fund world.

Paul, the techno geek of the partners, asked to see

the now infamous trading floor that was powering this enterprise. Tom was more than happy to oblige.

"Wow, Tom, really incredible what you've built here in such a short period of time. Great to be officially in business," Jim exclaimed as the partners gathered around Tom at the trading desk. Paul was practically drooling as he examined all of the technology, while Katharine scanned the faces of the associates and was reassured to see the bright eyes of confident, engaged people at work. Tom pointed out the key features of the trading desk and introduced them to the team.

After the intros, Tom walked them through the manufacturing area and then out to the loading docks, where several trucks were just heading out to make deliveries across the country. As they walked, Tom explained the process to Jim, Katharine, and Paul. "We decided to set up two different auction formats – one for consumers and one for retailers. Consumers can purchase cases of 24 bulbs and retailers can purchase a full truckload."

"What kind of pricing are we getting?" Paul asked, always wanting to stay on top of the numbers.

"Averaging $5 per bulb for cases and about $2.5 per bulb for full truckloads. Our best information suggests that the bulbs are selling for up to $7 at retail, but that's really not our concern."

"And volumes?"

"For the first week, we were selling individual cases like hotcakes, but those orders have slowed and the volume is shifting to the full truckload option. Fine with me, since it is much easier to manage logistically. We just send out the truck instead of packing and shipping hundreds of separate orders."

"The auction idea is brilliant, I must say," Katharine commented.

"It is working well so far. We bought a lot of equipment for the factory via auctions, so seemed to make sense to sell our bulbs as well. Fastest and simplest way to find the market price," Tom explained.

"How are you getting all of the traffic to the auctions?" Katharine asked. "Especially since no one had ever heard of this company until a few weeks ago?"

"Social media, not old school media. The old school approach would have cost us millions in airtime. But as soon as the repeal bill was signed, we were ready to go with a social media campaign."

"Oh, of course. I saw the YouTube ads get tweeted about," Paul nodded.

"Exactly. We shot a series of short videos announcing the availability of 100, 75, 60 and 40 watt incandescent bulbs, made right here in the USA – with no mercury," Tom explained.

"So how did it spread so fast?" Katharine wondered.

"We have a marketing expert at the auction desk – her job is to do whatever it takes to generate buzz for the company. We started with everyone we could find who had posted anything about the Baby Zoe video. Plus we ran some Google and Facebook ads just to grease the wheels. Pretty soon the word was out that we were the only game in town to get light bulbs."

"And now business is really brisk," Paul was practically giddy.

Tom nodded, "To say that business is brisk is a

complete understatement."

"This auction system is working brilliantly. Since the ban was repealed just four weeks ago, sales have surpassed the entire initial investment in the plant," Jim added.

Yes, the auction system was working brilliantly, Tom thought. Perhaps too brilliantly. And that was what was making Tom nervous.

CHAPTER 26

TJ Enterprises Factory, Charleston, South Carolina

"There you are, Tom, we've been trying to reach you on the walkie-talkies," the sales specialist exhaled as Tom and the investors returned to the auction desk.

"Sorry, we were touring the plant and warehouse. Must not have heard it with all the noise out there. What's going on?" Tom asked.

"Here, check this out. Looks like the spin machine is starting to gear up against us."

Tom and the investors gathered around as the specialist cued up the video on one of the flat panel displays. After a few seconds, the hokey patriotic theme music of Crossline came through the speakers and the announcer began.

"Bob Jenkins here with a special segment on what some are calling an emerging scandal – price gouging for light bulbs. Elaine Mitchell is here to give us the scoop. What's going on now?" Bob asked.

"Really disturbing, Bob. Really disturbing," Elaine sighed. "We are getting reports of incandescent light bulbs selling for up to $7 dollars each.

"Where are these bulbs coming from? Who's selling them?" Bob asked.

"Some fly-by-night outfit out of South Carolina," Elaine explained. "They sprung up out of nowhere and are selling light bulbs via the Internet."

"And how are they getting away with selling these bulbs at these prices?"

"Great question, Bob. Great question. I talked to my own grandmother just the other day – she wanted to buy some bulbs to stock up for a while – and she's just beside herself over these prices. It's really an outrage." Elaine looked smugly into the camera and then Crossline went to commercial break.

Tom looked in frustration towards Jim, Katharine, and Paul, "Great, now we are a fly-by-night price gouger. How do you like that?"

"I love it – check out our auction activity and pricing in the fifteen minutes since that segment aired!" Paul pointed to the screen, showing a surge in volume.

"I guess there's no such thing as bad publicity," Katharine joked, half-heartedly.

"Look, Tom, this stuff is just par for the course. Just stay focused and this will all blow over," Jim patted Tom on the back. "Come on, let's go play some golf. You deserve a break."

Tom thought about it for a moment, but then declined. "Thanks, but no thanks. I need to evaluate our readiness for an additional production line and stay in front of any of this potential fallout. You guys have fun."

Just as Tom walked them out of the lobby door into the parking lot, a couple of black SUVs pulled up. Eight men exited the vehicles and established a small perimeter in the parking lot. One of the men stepped forward, recognizing Tom immediately. He approached and presented his identification as a

U.S. Marshal from the Charleston field office. Tom inspected his badge and then asked "How can I help you?" as his investors looked on.

The marshal said, "I just need to give you this." He handed him a formal looking document.

As he unfolded the document, Tom realized that his captain's instincts had been right on.

Katharine noted the look on Tom's face, "What is it, Tom?"

"A subpoena to appear in front of the congressman's subcommittee for investigation on price gouging. Hearings are set to begin next week."

CHAPTER 27

Washington, D.C.

"Scandalous, Bob, just scandalous. That's the word to describe this morning's hearings," Elaine Mitchell reported from the Capitol steps. Elaine had lobbied the Crossline producer to let her cover these hearings live, even though technically she was a contributing analyst and not a reporter. She wanted to maximize the chance to shape the messaging around these events for her client.

"Give us a quick run-down of the key developments," Bob Jenkins replied from the network studio.

"Let's start with the damning evidence of outrageous price gouging. Check out this exchange with Mrs. Jane Holloway, a widow from upstate

New York." The producer cut from Elaine to a clip from the morning hearings.

The congressman removed his glasses, leaned forward, and in his most heartfelt, sympathetic voice, stated, "Now let me get this straight, Mrs. Holloway, ma'am. You had to pay $8 *per bulb?"*

Mrs. Jane Holloway was dressed in her Sunday best for the opportunity to testify to the United States Congress. She'd even had her hair done, just for the occasion. Her 83-year old voice cracked and trembled as she spoke into the microphone. "Yes, sir. I'm always just trying to make ends meet on my fixed income. Now I can't believe what I have to pay for light bulbs."

"Ma'am, thank you for being here today. I'm so sorry that you've had to experience this price gouging – it is simply unconscionable. I assure you that we will get to the bottom of this manipulation and restore stability and order to the light bulb supply," the Congressman replied in a gentle, supportive tone.

"So you see, Bob, a really tough morning," Elaine resumed her commentary.

"Tragic, Elaine, just tragic. So what's on deck for

this afternoon?" Bob asked.

"The main witness is the man selling these bulbs, Tom Jackson."

CHAPTER 28

"This place is a circus," Jim whispered to Tom as he slipped into the vacant seat next to Tom in the hearing room. Representatives, staffers, and observers were milling about, waiting for the afternoon session to begin.

"Hey Jim, what are you doing here? Don't you have a business to run? At least one of us could be productive today," Tom said. He had arrived early for the hearings dressed in a new blue pin-striped suit and a silver tie. With his athletic build and Captain's demeanor, Tom certainly attracted attention when he walked into the room. He took a seat in the observation area and settled in, waiting for his turn to testify. Tom sat through the morning testimony, grabbed a quick lunch, and then came back early to watch the various staffers filter into the hearing room, some laying out materials for particular representatives. The congressman milled about the room, seeming to work the crowd like a campaign event. Tom knew that he was in dangerous waters.

"No worries. Quick flight down and back from New York. I figured you could use someone in your corner. Besides, if our investment is going down in flames, I may as well at least enjoy the show," Jim laughed.

"Thanks, I appreciate it. Based on this morning's testimony, I'm clearly the underdog here." Tom spoke quietly so as not to be overheard.

"You fly up last night?" Jim asked.

"No, actually I brought your boat up. I do my best thinking out on the open water, so I decided to cruise up here along the coast and prepare for my testimony along the way."

"So are you ready for this?"

"Ready as I'll ever be. I had a few run-ins with top brass during my Navy career. Most of them were straight shooters, but a few were really political snakes. Figure I'm dealing with the same animal here," Tom explained.

"Be careful you don't get bit," Jim warned.

"Thanks, I'm not so worried about him." Tom nodded in the direction of the congressman at the center of the dais.

At that moment, Elaine Marshall entered the hearing room. Tom instantly recognized her from television, as he'd seen her countless times in the run up to today's events. He couldn't help but stare as she walked across the hearing room to find a seat in the galley. She looked even more beautiful in person. Clearly she knew a lot of people in this town, as every other person stopped her to chat. Tom was still watching her as she finally sat down and pulled a notebook and pen out of her bag. She looked up and noticed Tom watching her. Tom did not look away, but rather smiled and gave a slight nod as if to say hello. She returned the gesture.

Tom turned back to Jim, "Now she – is someone to worry about."

CHAPTER 29

The congressman took his seat in the center of the elevated platform and pounded the gavel. Once he could see that the red lights on the television cameras were lit indicating they were live, the congressman lowered his glasses and sneered down towards the main witness sitting at the table.

"Good afternoon, Mr. Jackson." He paused, looked down and shuffled some papers. "You have a very interesting story. I'm curious to know, how does a person go from chasing pirates to chasing profits?"

Tom had been expecting at least some opening pleasantries before the direct attacks began, so he was surprised by the immediate condescension in the congressman's question. Tom took a deep breath, and responded professionally and directly.

"Thank you, Congressman for inviting me to your hearings. As you may know, I recently retired from the United States Navy as a Captain, with my last command leading an anti-piracy task force."

Tom paused, giving the congressman a look that indicated he would not be a passive doormat like other witnesses. "I am not the type of person to sit around in retirement and quickly found an opportunity for leadership in the private sector. I am an entrepreneur and created a manufacturing company that currently employs 278 people – in jobs that pay well above the median level in our area. And we are hiring."

The congressman pushed his glasses back up, "Yes, I see you were also on the promotion list for Admiral – but then you were removed – so you retired instead. Apparently you have a bit of a reputation for pushing the rules of engagement. Care to explain what happened?" The Congressman pressed.

Son of a bitch. Tom was seething inside. The congressman was way out of line, not only leaking classified information about the Somali pirate capture but twisting it as well.

"Congressman, I'm not sure of the source of your information and I further question whether it is appropriate to disclose it in this setting. I will say, as I said many times to my superiors in the Navy, that I found the rules of engagement unnecessarily restrictive and ultimately ineffective in deterring pirates. So I declined the promotion and opted to return to private life."

"So what would you recommend? Execution at sea? Have them walk the plank?" The congressman smirked and leaned back in his seat, enjoying the titters that rippled through the hearing room.

Tom was growing tired of the veiled threats and accusations and decided it was time to go on offense. Time to break the pattern.

"Excuse me, Congressman." Tom interrupted, tapping on his microphone.

"Yes?" The Congressman replied.

"I am a private citizen with a business to run. I am no longer in the Navy and not prepared to discuss US and international policy on pirates, nor is it my understanding that such policy is the focus of this committee. Would you please dispense with the pleasantries and speechmaking and get to your questions related to the scope of this hearing? I would like to complete my testimony and get back to the business of producing light bulbs. I can assure you that my customers and employees would all appreciate it."

The staffers in the hearing room perked up like a bunch of meerkats on the plain who just spotted a lion. What was this? A different kind of animal was now in their territory. Not knowing where to run to, they froze.

"Very well, Mr. Jackson." The congressman was visibly annoyed by this request and responded in kind. "Before we begin, I must say that I am surprised to see you have no legal counsel with you? Also no sidecart full of binders and documents, which most executives bring along when they testify before this committee. Are you sure you are prepared for this hearing?" The congressman asked.

"Congressman, I appreciate your concern, yet I do believe that I am prepared for this hearing and am adequately represented. Please begin," Tom replied.

CHAPTER 30

"Well, let's begin, then, shall we?" the congressman started. "As you know, I have serious concerns about the excessive prices that you are charging for light bulbs, of all things, during a time of national vulnerability and about the extreme windfall profits that you appear to be reaping. So I intend to explore that issue at length to ensure that the interests of the American people are protected."

Tom waited patiently and said nothing, biding his time. He knew that the congressman was running a tried and true play, berating corporate executives who were expected to sit quietly and take their lumps.

"But before we get into these issues of price gouging, er... *potential* price gouging ..." The congressman paused for effect, allowing his accusation and then qualification to float in the air. "We need, well, the American people, need to understand that these recent developments appear to be part of a pattern on your part." The congressman paused and peered down at Tom over the bridge of his glasses.

Tom continued to wait for a question, knowing that these hearings were not about questions. They were about theater. The staffers and journalists were all watching to see Tom flinch. But it wasn't going to happen.

"What is your question, sir?" Tom asked.

The congressman was visibly perturbed by the interruption and repeated his insinuation, "As I was saying, before we even get to the price gouging and windfall profits, let's take a look at your original decision to sell incandescent light bulbs in the first place, which I believe would be an illegal violation of the *Energy Independence and Security Act*. I think the American people need to see just who we are dealing with."

While the hearing room audience saw this statement as a stinging attack, Tom took the comment in stride, noting that the Congressman still hadn't asked an actual question. Remembering his days as all-star linebacker, Tom knew he had just rattled the quarterback. His interruptions had penetrated the line of scrimmage just enough to tag him and let him know he was there, and the quarterback was now on edge. Just a matter of time before he would make a serious mistake.

Yet the Congressman mistakenly interpreted Tom's pause as weakness and indecision. "Perhaps you'd like to reconsider your decision to retain counsel. Of course, as many witnesses before Congress have done in these cases, you of course could invoke your rights under the fifth amendment to not testify to avoid self-incrimination?" Just to pile on, he added, "Or a brief recess to collect yourself?"

But Tom was calm and collected as always. He gently began to parry the Congressman's comments. "No, sir, that will not be necessary. But I'd ask you to consider, are you sure you want to proceed with this line of questions? You are making quite an accusation. I'd hate to see you expose yourself here."

The Congressman bristled at this remark, "Mr. Jackson, surely you know that we have immunity here in Congress – all part of the legislative process."

"Of course, but you do not have immunity from looking foolish. So let's talk it out, right here and let the American people decide."

The Congressman was now squirming in his seat. His normal tactics were backfiring and he'd just lost control of his own hearing.

Tom calmly and coolly began, "Let's consider your thinly veiled accusations against me of violating the law. First of all, under the *Energy Independence and Security Act* that you just referenced, incandescent bulbs are not illegal to make, only to sell. So for the entire time of my business prior to the repeal, the bulbs were not for sale. Not a single bulb was ever offered for sale. Thus how could a crime possibly be committed?"

"And second, let's suppose for just a moment that bulbs were sold. If that were the case, would there not be a federal indictment coming from the executive branch via a grand jury? Not from you here in Congress. Perhaps you should call them before this committee and ask why no indictment has been issued. Maybe they can explain to you not only that no crime was ever committed but also clarify for you the difference between the legislative and executive branches of our government." Tom stopped and waited for the words to sink in.

The Congressman was shocked into a stunned silence. All eyes were on him to see what he would do. Before he could speak, Tom intervened again. "Perhaps you'd like a brief recess to collect yourself?" The room erupted in laughter.

The congressman realized he was losing this round and deflected. "Yes, perhaps it would be good for all parties to calm down. Given the hour, we'll adjourn for the day and reconvene first thing in the morning." He pounded the gavel and sent a glare in Tom's direction.

CHAPTER 31

"Elaine, it looks like you've got front row seats at the hottest show in town. This Tom Jackson sure has ignited a firestorm," Bob Jenkins spoke from the network studio.

"Yes, Bob, it's really remarkable. Yesterday's hearings went viral across the web. Despite the overwhelming evidence, Tom Jackson actually seems to have some fans. Here's one tweet 'Finally we see a CEO willing to stand up for himself in a hearing. Go Tom!'" Elaine replied from the Capitol steps as the camera showed the crowd. "People are lined up trying to at least get a glimpse and hopefully a seat."

"Thanks, Elaine. We are going to be covering these hearings live throughout the day. We haven't done that since Oliver North and the Iran-Contra hearings in 1987," Bob Jenkins replied. "Looks like they are getting underway now."

As the second day of hearings opened, several networks were covering it live in a split screen and financial news services were streaming it into trading floors. With all of the tweeting and retweeting, the audience was growing exponentially. Across the country, people were gathered around laptops and televisions and iPads watching the action.

The hearing room was packed, standing room only. All of the committee members were now present as well and all of their staffers.

"Mr. Jackson, I hope that we can resume these hearings with an air of proper decorum and get right to the issues at hand," The congressman opened.

Tom nodded, noting the complete lack of any responsibility from the congressman, but was nonetheless content to move on. The sooner he was out of here, the better. Besides, there really was no way the congressman would be prepared for what would happen next.

"Mr. Jackson, let me be direct and get to the heart

of the matter. It appears to me and to this committee that your company is gouging people by charging excessive prices for light bulbs. You are nothing more than a heartless speculator reaping windfall profits based on your monopoly position in the industry. How do you respond?"

"Thank you for being direct. In the spirit of maintaining proper decorum, I would be more than happy to address your concerns. I just have one request in order to be able to do so," Tom stated.

"Go ahead," the congressman replied.

"I will need your assistance to define many of the terms in your previous statement so that I understand precisely what you mean by them, such that I can give a complete and truthful response. So if I ask you what terms mean, are you willing to define them?" Tom asked.

The Congressman smiled nervously. He sensed a trap, yet how could he not agree to such a polite request? "Yes, of course."

"First, could you tell me what you mean by excessive?" Tom asked.

"Well, you heard the testimony earlier this

morning. Some people were paying up to eight dollars per bulb for your light bulbs. *Per bulb!* For what is essentially pennies worth of glass and metal. How can you not call that excessive?"

"Congressman, did you stop at Starbucks this morning on your way into the hearing?"

"Yes, I do every day."

"And what did you order?"

"My usual. A venti caramel macchiato. Skinny." The room tittered with laughter, since the congressman's belly bore no resemblance.

"And how much did you pay for this beverage?" Tom asked.

"Five dollars and nineteen cents. What's your point?" The congressman asked.

"Wouldn't you say that is excessive? I mean, five dollars and nineteen cents for some brewed coffee, water, milk, and a bit of syrup?"

"Well, it's not just the ingredients, it's the preparation. Besides, it's my daily pleasure. To me, it's well worth it." A few people in the room clapped in agreement.

"And did anyone hold a gun to your head and force you to buy this venti … caramel … uh, macchiato?" Tom paused and then added, "Oh yes … skinny?" A cackling laugh came from a staffer behind the representatives. The congressman glanced back over his shoulder, then looked at Tom and shook his head.

Tom continued. "No, of course not. Just like no one was forced to buy light bulbs from my company. Every single light bulb that we have sold was purchased voluntarily, through a transparent auction system. Every person decided on their own what the bulbs were worth to them. So to address the first part of your charge, who is to say whether any price paid voluntarily is 'excessive'? If anyone determines that the price of a Starbucks Venti Caramel Macchiato – Skinny, or a light bulb from my company is excessive, then they simply do not have to buy them."

The congressman started to rebut, but Tom had seized the momentum and wasn't about to let go of it.

"Now as to whether I am a speculator. We all are speculators, are we not? Nothing in life is ever guaranteed. We all make bets in our lives about where to live, what careers to pursue, who to marry, what work to do – all based on our own desire and thoughts about what will bring us happiness. And do not forget that in every stock trade, there is a buyer and a seller. One is speculating it will go up, the other that it will not."

"So yes, I am a speculator. Guilty as charged – but let's define what that means. One day I went shopping for light bulbs for my home, learned that I could no longer choose to purchase an incandescent bulb. So I *speculated* that *eventually* the American public would see the ridiculousness of such a prohibition and *eventually* overturn it."

The congressman huffed, "Well, that is certainly a quite unusual perspective on speculation."

"Now when you speak of windfall profits, you are somehow suggesting that they came by luck or were unearned. Is that what you are suggesting, congressman?" Tom asked.

The congressman did not respond, so Tom continued.

"Despite the barriers and obstacles, I decided to invest time, energy and money in this venture to manufacture incandescent bulbs. I got other people, both investors and employees, to believe in the idea and then commit their time, energy, and money to this entrepreneurial venture. We placed a bet – as speculators – that ultimately we would have a business, but with no idea about when that would be. Many people at the time thought we were totally crazy, yet we proceeded anyway."

"Once the law did change, we were then in a position to grow our business, to sell our product to a market that wants to buy it. People are paying prices that you call excessive, yet they pay them freely and those sales provide a return on our original investment. So based on this information, congressman, would you still say that our profits are unearned? A windfall?" Tom asked.

All eyes and cameras turned to the congressman. With a sheepish look on his face, he responded. "Perhaps my use of the term windfall was a bit strong." Tom nodded in appreciation of the retraction, as lame as it was.

But the Congressman quickly shifted in tone, trying to regain some footing in his own hearing. "Yet Mr. Jackson, clearly you cannot dispute the fact that you have a *de facto* monopoly in this market." He smugly looked around the room, thinking he'd just landed a stinging rebuke.

"Yes, Congressman, you do make a good point. Let me explain. In a well-functioning, open and competitive market, other suppliers would see the supposed "excessive" prices that my company is getting for bulbs. Then they would quickly enter the market, add to the supply of bulbs available, and then the prices would come down. In fact, the higher the prices, the faster they would move, wouldn't you agree?"

"Sure, that's basic supply and demand at work," The Congressman answered.

"So then why do you think that no other suppliers have entered the market? Why do we have this *de facto* monopoly position in this market?" Tom asked the Congressman.

"Why don't you tell me?" The Congressman replied.

"Very well. You see, it costs a lot of money to build a factory, set up suppliers, hire employees, train them, and get a production line working properly. Make sense?" Tom asked.

"Yes, of course."

"So if you were going to invest in a factory like this and invest all of these resources, what would you want?" Tom asked.

"I'm not sure I follow your question, Mr. Jackson. Please just get to your point," the Congressman responded.

"Nearly every business owner I know or can think of, faced with such a decision, would want to make sure that they could generate a return on their investment. And the key factor in this case is one thing. Time."

"Time?"

"Yes. Time to sell products into the market, recoup the investment, and then generate a return. There's only one problem in this case."

"What's that, Mr. Jackson?"

"You didn't give them enough time. When the legislation to repeal the ban and legalize incandescent bulbs was introduced a few months ago, you insisted on a provision to make the repeal temporary. A one year repeal, not a permanent repeal. You introduced this so-called compromise with great fanfare, if I recall. So let's say it would take several months minimum to retool a plant and get it up and running. Then that leaves with you only a few months at the most to recoup your investment, much less make a profit, before your product becomes illegal again. So what company in their right mind would make such an investment to enter the market?"

The congressman looked completely stunned. But Tom wasn't finished.

"So my question is to you, Congessman. Why don't you take advantage of your own hearing to explain to the American people why you are personally responsible for bringing about the very monopoly that you now are criticizing?"

CHAPTER 32

Elaine watched the congressman's face turn beet red with embarrassment and then into rage. He seemed to be counting to ten internally to maintain his composure, looking down at his notes. Then he removed his glasses and stared straight at Tom. "These hearings are in recess until 9 o'clock tomorrow morning. I am not finished with you yet." With that, he banged down the gavel, gathered some papers under his arm and stormed out of the hearing room.

Elaine felt a wave of revulsion ripple through her body as she watched her mentor explode in front of a national audience. Two minutes later Elaine's phone was ringing. The congressman. "Meet me in thirty minutes in our usual local spot." Then he hung up.

The usual spot was the Johnny Rocket's in Union Station, about ten minutes from the Capitol. The station was busy with commuters but the restaurant was actually pretty quiet. The congressman was seated in the back corner when Elaine arrived, scarfing down a bacon cheeseburger. He didn't get up or offer Elaine anything, merely grunted and pointed with his forehead to the seat across from him. Elaine slid into the booth. As soon as he finished that bite of burger, he took a swig of Diet Coke, then looked up to her.

"Can you believe that guy? Made me look like a fool. In my own damn committee." He was clearly fishing for sympathy.

Elaine was careful, "Yes, I would say that today was not your best moment."

"I'm under pressure that you can't possibly imagine, Elaine. The switchboards at my office and at 1600 Pennsylvania Avenue are lit up with people complaining about these hearings."

"Complaining how?"

"Well, split. Some cheering us on, complaining about high prices for light bulbs, but frankly, most people want us to leave Tom alone."

Elaine pushed a bit here, "And the problem with that is what, exactly? He actually seemed pretty logical to me today." She noted the look on his face. "Sorry, I'm just looking at how this is going to play in the shows tonight. After your outburst, we need to do some damage control."

"Elaine, the problem is they just don't get it. This situation is much bigger than Tom. According to our good friend and your best client, sales of compact fluorescents are really down since this whole episode started. Not just down, way down. As in pretty much non-existent. Some people are paying the high prices for incandescents and others are simply waiting for more supply to come on line. Whatever the reason, they aren't buying CFLs. All of our progress over the past couple of years hangs in the balance and your client's business is in the ditch."

"So what are you going to do? And why am I here?" Elaine cut to the chase.

"Let's just say that things are going to get extremely unpleasant for Mr. Jackson." He noted Elaine's look of concern. "All above board, of course – but if Tom Jackson wants to play hardball with me, he is in for a rude awakening. We've worked too hard for too long to let one guy stop us. We need to let the American people know who is in charge."

"I'm not sure about this, Congressman. Why not just quietly end the hearings and let this whole thing fade away? Tom's only got a few months left anyway before the temporary repeal expires. Then our CFL friends are back to being the only game in town."

"Not that simple, Elaine. Now that people have a taste for these bulbs again, the voices are growing to make this repeal permanent. There are half a dozen bills and amendments in the works in various committees, not including mine, and those are only the ones I know about. You just go on camera tonight with your pretty face and keep spinning like you always do. You're the best at it. You do that and your business will just keep rolling right along."

Elaine did her best to contain her shock but her poker face failed her this time.

The Congressman polished off his burger and took a slurp of his soda. "Don't sit there looking so innocent, Elaine. What do you think we are playing, tiddlywinks? We are in a war, so start acting like it.

And don't forget whose side you are on. We are going to take down Tom Jackson and his company, too."

The Congressman pushed his empty plate away and studied Elaine. He could see that he'd been really hard on his protégé, so he tried to lighten the situation by turning on his charm. "Elaine, you know what amazes me the most about this whole situation? How this guy came completely out of nowhere. We've been working for years on making progress. When we cooked up this compromise repeal, we figured it would pacify all sides and buy us some time for people to forget about the whole thing. Then along comes Mr. Jackson and disrupts the whole plan. Until two months ago, no one in our circles even knew he existed. We just need to take care of him and his little venture and then everything will be back to normal."

Elaine stood up to leave, "Alright, Congressman, I've got to go prepare for tonight's shows. Keep me posted so I know what I'm spinning.

CHAPTER 33

What does he mean, "things are going to get extremely unpleasant for Mr. Jackson?" Elaine wondered as she walked out of Union Station back towards the Capitol and onto the National Mall. Tourists were milling about and a number of locals were out for their evening jogs.

Elaine felt like she'd kept the congressman at bay, but inside, she was totally lost. Thoughts were swirling in her head and she was starting to feel ill. He's always been such a good guy, advancing the cause of progress, and I owe my entire career and business to him. He launched my business for me with one phone call. Don't I owe him now, even though he made a total fool of himself today? Certainly he'll calm down by the morning.

Who am I kidding? He's not going to take this

lying down. I know the ruthless political hardball he's played over the years, and Tom Jackson crossed him good. When he said he's going to take Tom down, he looked like a cat against the wall ready to strike.

And then there's Tom Jackson, she thought as she passed the Washington Monument. I'm certainly no fan of CEOs, but Tom actually seems like a decent, reasonable guy. Strong and gracious, in fact, stating his case with total confidence and peace in spite of the clearly hostile environment that he found himself in. He must be some kind of man to be able to do that. Not only did he have presence, but some of what he said actually made sense. It was like seeing a big dog up close for the first time, after having been told your entire life to stay away from them, only to find out that the dog is not so bad after all. Not that it can't bite, but that its primary instincts are to love and protect. I don't know quite what to make of it, but I do see that the congressman is out to destroy Tom, at the behest of his corporate cronies, just to maintain his grip on power.

As she reached the reflecting pool, she stopped to take a good long look at herself. She was due to appear on Crossline in an hour. What was she going to say?

Elaine, it's time get real, she told herself. She continued down to the Lincoln Memorial, climbed the main steps, and then sat at the footsteps of the statue of the 16th president. She looked up into Lincoln's gaze, immortalized in stone, and prayed for wisdom.

After a few moments of silence, she came to a point of clarity. It's not about the congressman now, it's about me. What am I willing to do? Or not do?

And now she knew. As much as she cared about progress, how could progress be justified if it meant trampling on individuals like Tom Jackson? Clearly there must be a limit and she had found it for herself.

But for now, she needed to buy some time and to somehow find Tom. Unfortunately, that meant one last appearance on the news shows to maintain the spin for the congressman. If she didn't show or wasn't spouting the usual lines, he'd know something was up. That thought made her stomach churn.

CHAPTER 34

Washington, DC studios of Crossline

"Who does Tom Jackson think he is to show such disrespect to the institution of Congress and one of its esteemed committee leaders?" Elaine ranted for several minutes, boldly predicting that tomorrow's hearings would put Tom in his place. She went so over the top that even Bob Jenkins seemed surprised.

As soon as she was through shooting the segment, she ran down the hall to the bathroom to vomit. One of the production assistants walked in and heard her retching.

"You ok?"

"Yes, must have eaten something bad. I'm alright, but don't think I'll be able to stick around for the next segment. Tell the producer for me," Elaine responded.

Elaine washed her face and tried to rinse the taste of bile out of her mouth. She looked in the mirror. She was so disgusted with herself but swore she was done. Now she had to find Tom and make things right.

She grabbed a cab and headed back to her apartment. On the way she called Eric up in Cambridge. He picked up right away.

"Hey, Elaine. Just saw you on TV. How the hell can you defend that congressman after what he tried to do to Tom Jackson? Have you completely sold your soul?"

"Look, Eric. I can't explain that right now, but it's not what you think. I really need a favor."

"Ok, what can I do for you?"

"I need to find Tom Jackson. Tonight. I figure he's somewhere in the city since he's in town for the hearings."

"Elaine, there are hundreds of hotels in DC. He could be anywhere."

"That's why I called you. I figured with all of the

databases you had access to, you could locate him."

"You know I'm not supposed to do that, Elaine. "

"Eric, I'm sorry to ask you to do this, but all of us are over the line right now. I'm trying to make things right."

"Let me see what I can do. Give me a few minutes and I'll call you back."

CHAPTER 35

Alexandria, Virginia

After a quick shower at her apartment to wash off the grime of the day, Elaine threw on a pair of jeans, a black sweater, and running shoes. She pulled her hair back into a ponytail and put on a baseball cap. Then she packed a small suitcase, gathered up her laptop, cellphone and all the various chargers and accessories, and then waited. A few minutes later she got a text from Eric with the location of Tom's hotel, including the room number, 227. How he found it she could only guess. Maybe he accessed the credit card system or travel reservation system. In any case, she had the information she needed.

Elaine started to head to the hotel, but detoured and spent an hour circling the city and its monuments, contemplating what she was about to do. Finally she arrived at the hotel, checked her makeup in her car's vanity mirror one last time, and then noted the clock on her dash. It was just after midnight.

Elaine got out of her car, locked it, and then walked into the hotel lobby. She nodded to the desk manager and walked confidently through the lobby like she knew exactly where she was going. Any uncertainty would draw unnecessary attention to her visit. She found the elevator bank around the corner and was soon on the second floor, standing in front of Tom's room.

Elaine took a deep breath. She knew she was about to cross the point of no return. For a girl used to being in control of everything, she now had a feeling of both uneasiness and excitement.

She raised her fist and knocked on the door, "Mr. Jackson?"

No answer.

Elaine knocked a second time, a bit louder, and the pressed her ear to the door. Still nothing. Finally she pulled out her cell phone, called the hotel's main number, and asked to be connected to Tom Jackson in room 227. She heard the room phone ring a couple of times and as soon as the phone was answered, she hung up and knocked on the door again.

Tom Jackson peered through the peephole and then quietly cracked opened the door. He was dressed in some Navy sweatpants and a tee shirt. As a commanding officer in the Navy, Tom had been awakened in the middle of the night on more than one occasion. He had learned how to go from full sleep to full focus in about two seconds.

"Mr. Jackson, I'm Elaine Mitchell."

Even in jeans and a ball cap, Elaine was stunning. "I know who you are, Ms. Mitchell. The question is, why are you here?"

"I really must speak with you."

"Why? I saw you on television tonight. Why would I possibly want to listen to you?"

"Look, I'm really sorry and I promise to explain. Can I come in out of the hallway for just a minute?"

Tom was leery, but relented and remained fully on guard. He remained standing and directed Elaine to the sofa in the sitting area across from the desk.

"Alright, Ms. Mitchell, one minute."

"Please, call me Elaine. I realize you have no reason to trust me, but I beg you, please listen. After the hearings today I learned that they are going to come after you really hard tomorrow. I felt like I had to warn you. Tonight's appearance on television was just maintaining appearances until I could speak with you."

"They are going to come after me in the hearings tomorrow? So what? I think I can handle that. I did today."

"No, not the hearings. It's bigger than that. Way bigger. I don't know exactly what they have planned, but it's going to be bad."

Tom was not sure where this was going, but could read enough in her body language to believe her. Something in her entire demeanor had changed and he felt like he could trust her. "Ok, Elaine. Call me Tom. Let's back up a minute here. This is crazy. I'm just in town for a hearing. Sure it's annoying, but in a few days it will be over and I'll be back in business."

"Tom, you don't appreciate the resources these people have at their disposal." Elaine stood and looked Tom in the eyes. "This afternoon I saw up close and personal, clearly for the first time in my life that they will stop at nothing. The words I heard were that things were going to become "extremely unpleasant" for you and your business. Tom, you and I are just pawns in this game of big money and big power. I think they are going to come after you and your factory."

"What do you mean, come after my factory? I've got 278 people down there."

"I'm not sure, exactly. But you saw how the congressman came after you in the hearings. No matter how logical and reasonable you appeared, he makes you out to be the villain. Plus it's personal now. You embarrassed him on national television."

"He embarrassed himself." Tom went to the closet and started packing up his bags. "Well, I can tell you one thing. If he's going to come after my people, he's going to have to come after me. I've got to get back there."

"That's what I thought you'd do. So I'm coming with you."

Tom looked up from his suitcase and straight at Elaine. "You've done enough just by coming here to warn me. Don't drag yourself into this – you'll ruin a promising career."

"Tom, I sat at the feet of Abraham Lincoln this evening and realized that my career is over. I can't keep doing what I'm doing, not if it means so-called progress at the expense of trampling on people. I simply will not do it. I contributed to getting you into this position. Now I'm going to help you get out of it."

"And how exactly do you intend to do that?" Tom asked.

"In the next twenty-four hours, the resources of the federal government and their allies in the media are going to come after you. You've got to get your story out. I don't know exactly how this is going to play out, but I know how to spin a story."

"So why don't you just stay here and manage it from here? No need to get tangled up with me in case things go south."

"Yes, I've thought about that, too. Tonight the congressman told me to remember whose side I'm on. I can't be on the fence here, Tom. If I'm helping you from the sidelines, you may wonder if I've really got your back." Elaine reached out and shook Tom's hand. "I want you to know that I'm all in."

CHAPTER 36

Interstate 95, Southbound, Virginia

"No way, Tom. I know you want to get back to your factory quickly, but you can't fly commercial. You'll never get past airport security if they are looking for you," Elaine advised.

"Ok, then, we'll have to take the yacht," Tom said, immediately noting the puzzled look on Elaine's face.

"It belongs to my investors," Tom explained. "Racing yacht, super-fast, with state of the art communications on board. Not as fast as flying, but we can at least monitor the media on our way down the coast. I brought her up from Charleston before the hearings and docked her in Norfolk."

"Ok, let's go," Elaine said.

Thirty minutes later, they were in Tom's rental car, heading to Norfolk. She looked over at him from the passenger seat, and then gazed out the window. In the middle of the night, the traffic on Interstate 95 heading south out of DC was minimal. The first half hour or so passed in almost total silence, with only minor chit chat. It seemed a bit awkward, yet strangely comfortable.

"So, Elaine, what's your story?" Tom figured they had about a three hour drive, so he may as well get to know his new partner in crime, if that was an accurate description. He listened as she told of growing up in California, going to top schools, her path to power in Washington, and how she now found herself in too deep. After a half hour or so, Tom returned the favor, recounting his path from Charleston to the Navy and then back, and now to DC.

Tom looked out the window as they passed the few cars on the road. He tried to make sense of it all. Two people who only hours before were on complete opposite sides of the issue were now conspiring fugitives. Well, not officially fugitives yet. But by morning they would be. And the line between a fugitive and a patriot was getting blurrier by the minute.

Elaine was really starting to like Tom, and vice versa. Yet Elaine still could not understand this man, who up until a few hours ago was the monster personified at whom she directed all of her political energy.

"Tom, I do wonder about one thing. Ok if I ask?"

Tom laughed, "Just one? Sure, go ahead."

"I think I understand what you said in the hearings today. Well, yesterday. I'd never really thought about it from that perspective – you know, the auctions and everything, but it does make sense," Elaine paused. "I just don't understand why you are opposed to CFLs in the first place."

"I am not opposed to CFLs, Elaine. Never have been," Tom replied.

"Sure you are. You run a company that sells incandescents. How could you not be?"

"Elaine, I'm not opposed to CFLs. What I'm opposed to is being forced to buy them, or more precisely, to have my freedom to choose incandescent bulbs taken away."

"I'm not sure I fully understand, but go on. I've

been involved in this arena for years. Everything I've seen indicates that moving to CFLs is a really good policy in terms of saving energy and protecting the environment."

Tom's reply was gentle and patient, which surprised Elaine. Maybe she was expecting him to get riled up and frothy, but it didn't happen.

"From my perspective, my concerns are with the policy itself, the approach of the policymakers, and most importantly, the underlying principle at stake. Let's start with the policy," Tom said.

"Ok, let's hear it."

"I will agree with you that CFLs may be fine for many people in many circumstances. They last a long time and use less energy."

"Exactly."

"But many people in many circumstances does not mean all people in all circumstances. Sometimes a CFL doesn't really work the way you want it to and sometimes it poses risks that are simply not right for you. Let's say you have small children or pets. They like to get into things and a bulb breaks. Now the trace mercury in the CFL is in your carpet, on your furniture, on your children's skin. Do you want that?"

"No, of course not."

"So I think that while most people are in favor of protecting the environment – the environment they care most about is their immediate environment – their home. If they break, your immediate environment just got pretty bad, right? Not sure that's a tradeoff I'm willing to make."

"But doesn't it make society better off in the long run?"

"Well, let's consider the three bulb technologies on the market. We have incandescents, we have compact fluorescents, and now we have light emitting diodes (LEDs). Roughly speaking, before incandescents were outlawed, the price for these bulbs was around $1 for the incandescent, $4 for the CFL, and $14 for the LED. If you are really serious about energy efficiency and environmental protection, why not go all the way and outlaw the CFLs, too? Just set the standards so everyone has to buy LEDs?"

"But LEDs are really expensive." Elaine replied.

"Maybe, but compared to the benefits to society?" Tom asked, playing devil's advocate.

"But if that's your only option, that's a lot of money," Elaine responded.

"Exactly. Let's say you are a middle class family trying to raise kids, pay your bills, save for college, and maybe have some extra money for a vacation or even your own retirement. Now you have to spend $13 extra dollars on every light bulb in your house. Let's say it adds up to a few hundred dollars. Is that family really better off?"

"Ok, fine, but think of the savings in terms of energy."

"Perhaps, but energy is just one of many things that a person buys and just one of many resources in society. Let's say that this family takes that money and invests in their retirement savings so that down the road they are self-sufficient in retirement and not dependent on the state. Doesn't that make society better off? What if they use that money to send a kid to college and he becomes an entrepreneur who creates jobs for others? What if they use that money to simply buy food and clothing? Doesn't that make society better off?"

"Ok, I see your point. "

"So, these kinds of tradeoffs are everywhere for every type of product on the market. Maybe it's my background as an engineer, but it is pretty much impossible to create a product that is all things to all people in all circumstances – there are always tradeoffs in terms of quality, cost, performance, design … all sorts of factors. And these tradeoffs exist within a broader context of someone's life."

"Sorry, Tom, you lost me there."

"Let's try a different example. What kind of cell phone do you have?" Tom asked.

"An iPhone, of course."

"What did you have before that?"

"A Blackberry."

"Why did you switch?"

"Oh, it's just so beautiful and wonderful to use."

"More expensive overall?"

"Maybe a bit more, but worth it."

"How did you decide it is worth it?"

"I don't know, I just did."

"So why not require everyone to get an iPhone."

"Well, that's ridiculous. There are hundreds of cell phones on the market and dozens of different plans."

"Why do you think that is?" Tom asked.

"Because people have different needs, wants, and budgets in terms of whether to get a cell phone at all, what kind to get, and how much they are willing to pay," Elaine replied.

"So how are light bulbs different?"

"Oh." Long pause. "Ok, ok. I get it."

"So that leads me to the concern about the approach of the policymakers," Tom continued. "Everything has tradeoffs. So if you are making law or policy here, how can you possibly know what technology is going to work best? For all people in all circumstances? How can you possibly know how people should spend their money?"

"What about the need to jump start innovation? Without this policy, we'd never move the technology forward?" Elaine asked.

"All the jump starting in the world doesn't change the laws of physics or supply and demand.

All the jump starting in the world doesn't change the fact that these CFLs have mercury. So jump starting in this case means forcing people to take a risk that they may not freely choose."

Elaine pondered for a moment.

"Look, Elaine, we could debate the policy issues all night long. But let's cut to the chase and deal with the bigger, more fundamental issue."

"Ok, what's that?"

"Freedom itself."

"Alright, I'm still listening."

"I'm willing to concede that maybe, just maybe, the legislation on CFLs might do some good overall in terms of energy savings. But, what we miss is what gets taken away in the process. Our freedom erodes. How does that make society better off? It's what Alexis De Tocqueville called 'soft despotism' – tyranny by a thousand cuts."

"So when I came back from the sea and realized I couldn't buy something as basic as a light bulb, I decided to build a factory just out of principle. I didn't care if I couldn't sell them for decades, if ever. But I was going to make them," Tom said.

"I'm really struggling with this, Tom. But I'm still listening. I mean, I did go to graduate school for many years on environmental policy. The people I've worked with have a lot of expertise on these issues. They have good intentions."

"Sure, I get that. But expertise is not omniscience. And even with good intentions, this kind of power ultimately corrupts people in their attempts to control every aspect of society. The founding fathers recognized this as a fact of human nature, which is why the constitution is designed to limit the power of the federal government."

Elaine nodded, "And I certainly saw that up close and personal today. Thank you, Tom."

They drove in silence for the last thirty minutes into the Norfolk area and into the marina. Tom hopped out of the car, grabbed his suitcase from the trunk, and headed down to the boat slip.

"Look, I appreciate your coming down here. If you want to turn around and head back to DC, I totally understand."

"What are you saying, Tom?"

"Just that I'm letting you off the hook. I

appreciate what you did to come find me, Elaine. But now that you've spent three hours face to face with the devil, I thought you might have changed your mind."

Elaine approached Tom and took his hands into hers, "Tom, I realize I just entered into a foreign territory." She smiled. "A lot of what you said tonight is new to me, but I get it. Just need some time to absorb it and figure it out. But then I think about the congressman and what he's prepared to do to maintain his power. That is no way to live. Tom, I get it, finally. I may end up in jail or dead by the time this is all over, but at least I have my freedom."

CHAPTER 37

Atlantic Ocean

By ten a.m., Tom and Elaine were out at sea heading south at a comfortable cruising speed. Elaine was amazed at the communications equipment on this yacht – high-speed satellite Internet access. She configured a variety of news feeds to display on the flat panel screens on the bridge. Now they were waiting for a pending press conference called by the congressman up in D.C.

The news cameras and reporters were assembled for what was billed as a "major announcement." At the congressman's insistence the night before, Elaine had pinged her media contacts to assure them that they did not want to miss this event. The place was packed and the major networks were covering the press conference live.

The congressman approached the podium and waited for the chatter to die down, and then waited a couple of moments more. All eyes were on him, not just in this room, but across the country and world. He lived for this stuff.

"Ladies and gentlemen, I have a very important announcement to make this morning that will restore fairness and sanity to the market for light bulbs." The congressman paused for effect before continuing.

"It is essential that all Americans can get the light bulbs that they critically need."

"But before I announce the specifics, I want to review the developments that have brought us to this point."

"Now as you know, my entire career has been focused on leading the way forward in terms of ensuring environmental protection and energy independence, and I've sponsored substantial legislation in this area."

"Over the past few months we have seen several challenges emerge that threaten to block our ongoing progress. After breakthrough legislation to promote energy efficiency through the adoption of more efficient compact fluorescent bulbs, the industry experienced a supply disruption that unfortunately caused a very, very small percentage of the American people to lose confidence in these bulbs."

Tom looked to Elaine, "Seriously? Who writes this guy's speeches?"

The congressman continued, "Based on the outcry from this vocal minority and despite my concerns that it would undermine our long term progress, we passed temporary repeal legislation to allow incandescent bulbs to return to the market."

"As we all have witnessed, this repeal created an opportunity for a ruthless speculator to create a monopoly and then charge outrageous prices for a household commodity. How can we tolerate the situations that we heard in the hearings, like our elderly citizens on fixed incomes being forced to pay almost $10 per bulb? Clearly this outrage cannot stand."

"But this issue goes beyond economic fairness and strikes at the heart of our national security readiness as well. How can we allow the supply of such an essential – *light itself* – to be at the whims of a single individual who is bent on extracting maximum profit from his fellow countrymen? And at the same time preventing people with legitimate needs from getting these bulbs?"

"So in consultation with the President, we have determined that this situation must be rectified. By executive order signed this morning, we are bringing the light bulb factory in South Carolina under federal supervision."

"Further, we recognize that we need experienced business leadership and have appointed an executive with extensive industry experience to serve as the Lighting Czar during this temporary period. He will take over the operations of the light bulb factory and make sure that it runs effectively. We thank him for answering the call to service during this critical time. We expect that within a couple of weeks we will have the light bulb pricing situation stabilized and the American people will be able to get the bulbs they need at prices that are fair."

Tom watched as the very executive who runs the CFL business and testified after the Baby Zoe affair was now standing beside the congressman. Elaine, of course, saw this same executive as her client, or now soon-to-be former client.

The congressman opened up for a few questions.

"What about Tom Jackson?"

"Currently Mr. Jackson's whereabouts are unknown. He failed to appear before my committee this morning and accordingly is facing charges for contempt of Congress. And, while it is perhaps premature to discuss, we are now considering Mr. Jackson as a person of interest in the original supply disruption."

The reporter begged for a follow-up, "What do you mean by person of interest?"

"Let me just say that I find it more than just a coincidence that the CFL supply is disrupted in such a way that it enabled his business plan."

CHAPTER 38

Atlantic Ocean

Elaine looked at Tom. See, I told you they would go after you, her eyes said. Sorry.

Tom was livid. "These reporters are useless sheep. Don't they have an independent thought in their brains? No one asks a single question about the authority of the federal government to "supervise" my factory. No one considers the idea that this is an unlawful seizure or outright nationalization of an industry, with a hand-picked crony to run it? Where is the fourth estate? Maybe we should just go ahead and change the Pledge of Allegiance to say 'to the Banana Republic' for which it stands."

Elaine touched Tom on the arm. The warmth of her touch calmed him instantly.

"Tom, aren't you even concerned that they are calling you a person of interest?" Elaine was shocked that he went immediately to the federal issues.

"No, not really. Why would I? I had nothing to do with that. I'm more concerned with the press. What use is freedom of the press if the press is in the tank for the politicians? They just go along. No one asks if the congressman has any evidence that would make me a person of interest?"

"Tom, look, I appreciate your idealism. But you've got to deal with this. They are going to come after you. It's just getting started."

Tom looked out to the horizon, took a sip of coffee, and then turned back to Elaine, "Alright, enough complaining. Let's get to work."

"So what do we do now?" Elaine was relieved by Tom's refocusing.

"Well, I need to take care of my team. I'm captain of this company and my primary responsibility now is to get back there. In the meantime, we've got to get some help to fight this person of interest thing."

"How?"

"I don't know. Know any good lawyers?"

Elaine laughed, "What are you kidding? I live in Washington. I know tons of them. The problem is they are on the other side. In either case, I'm afraid we may be beyond that."

"What do you mean?"

"This battle is going to be won or lost in the press, not in the courts. Sure, you will need some good legal help, but you've got to fight back in the press. They are going to try to shut you up and keep you out of the picture. Plus you've got to prove your innocence."

"Look, I know nothing about this supply disruption. We started the company based on a long term bet that the policy would eventually change. Are we glad that policy changed? Sure. Did we do something nefarious to bring it about? Absolutely not," Tom explained.

Elaine paused and considered the implications of what she was about to say. She had no idea how this would play out, yet there was no turning back. Tom noticed her hesitation.

"What, Elaine? Go ahead, say it," Tom said.

"Can you establish an alibi?" Elaine questioned, "To prove your innocence?"

"I don't know how to prove a non-event." Tom paced across the bridge and checked some instruments.

"I was just thinking, maybe we could just show that you weren't in those cities during any of those days along the sabotage path."

Tom turned back, "Wait a minute. What do you mean 'along the sabotage path?' I thought, hell, everyone thought, that there was just a manufacturing glitch. But sabotage? What do you know that you haven't been telling me?" Tom was clearly pissed, but contained.

Elaine started to cry, "Oh, Tom. I'm so sorry. I have a good friend – a computer geek – he figured out that there was a pattern in the breakages that clearly pointed to a saboteur – there is really no other explanation. I asked him to keep it quiet so I could spin it for my clients. I feel terrible. I never imagined that they would go this far."

Tom sighed and accepted the reality of the situation. He stepped across the bridge and brought her into his arms. "Elaine, it's ok. At least I know the truth now and we can deal with it."

"Really, you aren't angry?"

"Sure, for a moment, I contemplated throwing you overboard right here," Tom joked. "I learned a long time ago that anger doesn't really serve you when you need to focus. I just try to accept what is and deal with it." He handed Elaine a tissue and she dabbed the tears from her face.

"So what now?" Elaine asked.

"You still friends with this computer geek?"

"Well, sort of."

"Is he good?"

"Probably one of the best hackers on the planet."

"Get a hold of him. We've got to get him to track down the real saboteur."

"Sure, I'll contact him right away," Elaine said.

"And," Tom thought out loud, "I'm going to need his help with something else."

CHAPTER 39

Interstate 26 between Columbia and Charleston, South Carolina

Joel Bryant was heading southeast in his Ford F150 Extended Cab down Interstate 26 in the mid-morning hours. He took a sip of coffee and placed the big tumbler of coffee in the center console cup holder. Joel was on his way from Charlotte to Charleston to meet with a new customer for his engineering firm, so he scanned through his playlists looking for a particular motivational audio program on sales. He spent so much time in his car, he thought of it as a rolling library.

As he neared the outskirts of Charleston, traffic was still quite light. Joel was rehearsing his sales meeting out loud when he noticed the blue lights flashing behind him. He checked his speed. Sure, he was going a tad fast, but enough to get pulled over? Joel slowed and moved to the right lane.

A few moments later, a convoy of about a dozen black SUVs screamed past him. They were moving at a very fast clip and clearly not concerned with him. On a whim, Joel sped up to follow and noticed them taking an exit up ahead, so he pulled off as well. He paused his MP3 player and switched to the local AM radio, looking for news.

Joel watched as the SUV convoy pulled up to the gated parking lot of what appeared to be a manufacturing facility. Several large vans from various media outlets were already on the scene, their satellite antennae up and ready. Camera crews were out checking their gear and reporters were doing mic checks. Joel turned on his iPad tablet and pulled up the app for one of the news outlets, wondering if they would stream live whenever things started to break.

After about twenty minutes, the press conference was getting started. Joel could see it from a distance and up close from the streaming footage on his iPad.

From Joel's count, about twenty federal agents had established a perimeter around the parking lot.

He guessed they had been dispatched from the Columbia field office. In the middle of this assemblage, a man in his mid-fifties approached the microphones held by the reporters gathered outside the plant.

"As you know, today I have joined the administration as Lighting Czar. My mission is to correct a grave injustice perpetrated by a ruthless speculator and get the supply of light bulbs flowing to the American people at fair prices. Clearly I have a lot of work to do, so I will only have time for a few questions."

"What is your plan?" one reporter asked.

"Our first step is to make sure that the existing inventory gets out to the public quickly and gets allocated properly to customers who really need the bulbs – like hospitals, schools, government agencies, and seniors on fixed incomes. Second, we will look for ways to increase production rapidly and dramatically. In fact, I have a team of crack Six Sigma specialists arriving now to begin their analysis." He pointed across the parking lot where about a dozen consultants were emerging from rental cars, brushing off their suits and heading toward the building with their laptop cases slung over their shoulders.

"How have the employees reacted to this change?"

"I'm heading in to meet with them now. I suspect that in this economy, they will be thrilled to know that their jobs are secure," the executive responded.

Joel watched this statement and thought to himself, "Yeah, right."

CHAPTER 40

Atlantic Ocean

Out on the yacht off the North Carolina coast, Tom Jackson had a similar reaction as he and Elaine watched the executive's press conference. "Ok, Elaine, I know that can't be true. I know my people. Let's see what they have to say."

"What do you mean?"

"Well, if he's going in to talk with them, we should be able to watch the whole thing." Tom connected his laptop to the large flat screen display, opened up his Firefox browser, and selected a bookmarked page. A few seconds later, eight video players filled the screen. Tom selected one and waited.

"What's this?" Elaine asked.

"Like most industrial operations, we have cameras placed throughout our facility. I can access them through a web control panel."

"To monitor your employees?"

"Not really. I trust everyone who works in our company. Most of the time, we never even refer to the videos. Yet occasionally if something goes wrong on the line, we can pull the video and break down what happened. Kind of like having the game film from a football game," Tom explained.

"Can you get audio?"

"Sure. It's not the greatest, but it'll do."

Tom pulled up the main lobby video and studied the screen intently. The lighting czar executive and his entourage were clogging up the lobby. Tom turned up the volume on the speakers and could make out small talk among the consultants and federal agents clustered in the room. The reception desk was empty. The executive leaned against the reception counter while one of his minions knocked on the secured door that led from the lobby into the plant.

Elaine leaned against Tom, her hand on his back

as she looked over his shoulder. "Tom, this is a secured web page, right?"

"Yes, it is password-protected. Why do you ask?"

"Well, I was just wondering. What if we made it public? Why not let everyone watch what happens?"

"I'm not sure how this will play out," Tom replied.

"Of course not. But nobody will know what happens inside that plant otherwise. Let's at least get it out there."

Tom thought for a moment, and then nodded in agreement, "So how do we do it?"

"Simple. Can you remove the password protection?"

"Sure, give me a minute." Tom opened up a new window with the administrative console to his web system. After a few clicks, he turned to Elaine, "Done."

"Great, now all I need is the web address and I'll tweet it."

"Tweet?"

"Wow, Tom, you really have been out at sea too long. Twitter," Elaine explained, but Tom still looked confused.

"Look, I'll explain it to you later, but think of it like a short signal out to the world. Kind of a modern-day Morse code. I have a ton of followers, so someone will pick it up for sure."

A few seconds later, Elaine's tweet "Live video of federal light bulb supervision here http://bit.ly/NDpleA" went out to the world. Or at least her three hundred and seventeen thousand or so followers. The retweets happened almost instantly.

Tom watched her type out the tweet. "Supervision? Why don't you call it takeover?" Tom was getting agitated.

"Tom, I get it. But my audience does not. I want to make sure they pick it up."

Tom turned back to the video and watched. After a few moments, the secured door opened and woman in her early forties, dressed in coveralls, came into the lobby. Tom motioned to Elaine, "That's Gina – she's our director of operations. Former chief petty officer in the Navy. Looks harmless, but that's deceiving. She's one tough cookie.

"Good morning, sir. How may I help you?" she asked. Tom watched her scan the room and take a quick mental inventory of the group gathered in the lobby.

The executive spoke, "I would like to gather all employees together for an all-hands meeting right away. And my team here will need immediate and complete access to this facility. Oh, and some coffee would be nice."

"Yes, I'm sure it would. We'll get some coffee going right away. As for your other requests, I would need to check with Tom. Who are you, exactly?"

"Oh, I'm sorry, I thought you would have heard by now. I'm the new federal lighting czar. As of this morning, by executive order, this company and plant are now under the supervision of the United States Government."

He placed an official looking document on the counter. She picked it up, studied it for a moment, then handed it back.

"I'm sorry, sir, this plant is owned by Tom Jackson, our investors, and the employees of this company. So unless I hear from Tom, I'm afraid I will not be able to accommodate your requests."

"Ah, yes, ownership. What an interesting concept. I'm afraid you don't understand. We are in a national security crisis and must ensure that the lighting supply is secure. Rest assured that this is only a temporary measure." The executive gave a brief glance to the federal agent to his right, at which point six agents stood and moved closer to the reception counter.

The intimidation worked, as Gina realized her situation and suddenly became more compliant. "Yes, of course. Give me a minute." She picked up a phone at the reception desk, hit a few buttons, and then her voice emanated through speakers in the lobby and the plant. "Attention all hands. Cease all operations safely. All hands meeting in the cafeteria in ten minutes." The executive smiled smugly and the federal agents backed away slightly.

Elaine tapped Tom on the shoulder, "Check this out. Looks like a few of the networks are picking up the video." She pointed to the news streaming from a major network. It was mid-day, so they had three small screens embedded in the right hand side of the main screen as the news reader tracked various stories. "I bet they will cut in once the meeting starts. Yep, here they go. It's streaming live!"

CHAPTER 41

The employees of TJ Enterprises were gathered in the company cafeteria. Some sat, some stood. Most were silent. A few were making nervous small talk. The lighting czar stood on a small platform at one end of the room, flanked on both sides by federal agents and a small cadre of consultants in suits.

"Good morning, everyone," the executive began with a smooth tone and flashed a smile across the room. The assembled employees were instantly silent.

"Who here is on the warehouse and logistics team?" No hands moved. "We need to get the trucks loaded up and start moving inventory out of the warehouse. We have a few regional distribution centers set up to get these bulbs out to the public.

And the production team? We want you all to get the lines rolling so our great team of Six Sigma experts here can help make sure that our production processes are both efficient and in compliance with regulations. Then we'll have ourselves a kaizen day to brainstorm ways to increase production." The executive grinned, pleased with himself and his take charge approach.

There was no reaction from the gathered group. He scanned the crowd and asked, "Any questions?"

Silence.

"All right, then. Let's get back to work," The newly-anointed lighting czar announced to the assembled group.

Except nobody moved.

The executive conferred with some of his staff. One of the consultants suggested that he dust off his change management skills from a recent leadership seminar. He needed to overcome the resistance and get buy-in. The executive turned back to address the group again.

"I know you may be surprised to come to work today to encounter a change like this, but let me assure you that we all have the same mission here … to provide high quality lighting products to our customers. I know this change really may be a shock to many of you. But really nothing has changed; you all can go about your regular jobs."

The crowd of employees watched with blank stares as he continued, "You can all relax and know that your jobs are secure. Your wages and benefits are secure. Nothing really is going to change in terms of your day to day work."

Finally a young, junior employee in the back raised her hand. The executive pointed to her and she stood up to speak. The crowd of employees parted so she could be seen and now she was the center of attention.

"How can you say that nothing really has changed? Everything has changed."

"No, not really. You still have your same job. And it's even more secure now."

"Well, I'm not sure that I agree that it is more secure. But even if it is, I'm pretty sure I don't want that."

The lighting czar was stunned, "What do you

mean, you don't want that?"

"Security. Not if it means working under these terms. We have no problem with our wages. We are well paid and we have a stake in the business. We all came here to work with Tom to build a great company, not just to get a paycheck."

The executive was stunned. Never in his career had he seen this insubordination. He turned and nodded to one of the agents, who gave a quick grunt. The agents fanned out around the room, establishing a perimeter around the assembled employees.

"I appreciate your loyalty to Mr. Jackson and your concerns, but we've got a national security situation here. We need to get these trucks moving and ramp up production to get more light bulbs out to people. Got it?"

The young woman looked to one of her co-workers, who shook his head slowly. Don't push it, his eyes said. But she would not be contained.

"Well, then, I just have one more question," the young woman said.

"And that is?"

"So you are going to ship these bulbs out of our warehouse?"

"Yes."

"So why won't you just call it what it is?"

"And what's that?" the executive asked.

"Stealing."

Joel Bryant was still sitting in his Ford 150 Truck watching the video stream through to his iPad. The executive and the young worker were locked in a stare down. "Stealing. Damn straight."

Joel reached for his cell phone and placed a call. "Hey, Chris. You watching this stuff? Yeah? Can you hitch up your horse trailer and be ready to meet me on 1-26 just outside of town? I'll call you back with specifics." Joel hung up and placed several more calls.

CHAPTER 42

Washington, DC studios of Crossline

"Ladies and gentlemen, welcome to Crossline. Tonight we have a very special guest to discuss today's events. Welcome, Congressman." Bob Jenkins could not hide his excitement.

The camera panned back from the host to reveal the congressman seated at the opposite end of the news desk and with the background view of the U.S. Capitol.

"Thank you, glad to be here. I have an important announcement to make here tonight."

"Great, we are thrilled to carry it here live and exclusively. Let's start by getting your thoughts on an incredible day. The morning started with your announcement of the executive order placing TJ

Enterprises, the only supplier of incandescent light bulbs, under federal supervision. By this afternoon, the workers are reluctantly back on the job, but the trucks transporting the current inventory are stuck on Interstate 26 behind what appears to be a blockade set up by local citizens. What do you make of all of these events?"

As the host spoke, the screen switched to video footage of Interstate-26 westbound out of Charleston. Six tractor-trailers with the TJ Enterprises logo on the side were at a standstill on the highway. Just in front of them, a half-dozen pickup trucks and a couple of horse trailers were spread across the highway, blocking any movement. Traffic behind the trucks had built up for a few miles.

The congressman spoke, "Well, what started out as highly questionable, if not illegal, behavior by a ruthless speculator and monopolist has now turned into an illegal work slowdown by his workers and now an illegal roadblock set up by some yahoos intent on interfering with federal officials."

The anchor responded, "What about the employee who said that what is happening is effectively stealing?

"I'm not sure they realize just how selfish they are. They are the only people with the know-how to make these bulbs and now with their work slowdown they are holding the entire country hostage. We're dealing with a national security situation now. Same principle that Harry Truman used during a national security crisis to ensure steel production. These employees must ramp up their production so we can alleviate this crisis."

"What's the latest on your investigation into Tom Jackson?" Jenkins asked.

The congressman continued, "Well, as you can see, he has clearly created a culture in his company based on selfishness and greed, such that his employees would openly defy our reasonable and well-intentioned efforts to distribute light bulbs on a fair basis to the public."

"We are still investigating Mr. Jackson's connection to the original supply disruption that paved the way for the temporary legalization of his business. We are tracking his whereabouts during the time of those events."

"Where is he now?"

"Right now, we believe that Tom Jackson has fled Washington, D.C. and is out at sea in a private yacht, heading south along the coast. We also have some very disturbing news. We now believe that Mr. Jackson has actually kidnapped Elaine Mitchell, a great public servant who has done so much to advance the cause of energy efficiency and independence. We believe, based on our investigation, that Ms. Mitchell is a hostage aboard the private yacht – that is, assuming she is still alive."

"Oh my, that is quite a terrible development." The host could not contain himself. "I've known Elaine for a long time. Our viewers of course know her as one of our key contributors to this show. She's been on this show many times."

"So tonight I must announce that Mr. Tom Jackson, the ruthless monopolist and speculator who would hold regular Americans hostage to outrageous prices for light itself, has now crossed the line and is holding Elaine Mitchell hostage. Accordingly, Mr. Jackson is now #1 on the FBI's most wanted list."

"In consultation with the president, we've

ordered the US Coast Guard and Navy to capture Mr. Jackson at sea and secure the safe release of Ms. Mitchell."

PART III

"It is important to remember that government interference always means either violent action or the threat of such action. Government is in the last resort the employment of armed men, of policemen, gendarmes, soldiers, prison guards, and hangmen. The essential feature of government is the enforcement of its decrees by beating, killing, and imprisoning. Those who are asking for more government interference are asking ultimately for more compulsion and less freedom."

– Ludwig von Mises

CHAPTER 43

Atlantic Ocean

"Oh, my God, Tom. I cannot believe it. I never thought he'd go this far." Elaine jumped out of her chair on the bridge and walked to the railing and looked out to the water. The yacht was moving south at a steady clip.

Tom was speechless. America's most wanted? Not only was the business going down, but now he really might not make it out of this mess. He turned down the volume on the Crossline video stream and took a sip of coffee.

After a few silent minutes, Elaine walked back over to Tom, "You ok? We can fight this, Tom. These charges are crazy. If you are worried about having to go to prison, that's not really going to happen."

"Thanks for the optimistic outlook, Elaine, but that's really the least of my concerns at the moment. My people at the plant – you saw them on the video – they are so demoralized, working under this so-called supervision. Amazing how their spirits can be brought down in a blink of an eye. I really just want to get back to stand with them through this mess. I feel like I'm letting them down being out here."

Elaine tried to lighten the mood, "I understand, Tom. So how does it feel to be America's most wanted man?"

Tom laughed, "Comical. And tragic."

He took another sip of coffee. "You know, I spent years in the Navy, protecting freedom. When you are out at sea for months at time with nothing to do but think, you start to think about the nature of the thing you are defending. Freedom is a fragile thing. When the federal government tells you that you can't buy a simple light bulb, where does it end? When the federal government dictates the time and manner and price at which you may or may not sell what you produce, where does it end?"

"Whatever happens to me, I think we are starting to see where it ends." Tom got up to pace.

"What do you want to do? Turn yourself in?" Elaine asked. "We can get to shore and explain everything."

"Surrender? Hell, no. Don't you see what I represent to them? There is no way out."

"Ok, then what? Run for it?"

Tom laughed, "Outrun the Navy? Where do we run to? Besides, we don't have enough fuel to get past Miami. No, we must keep pushing to get back to the factory. Regardless of how this turns out, I will go stand with my team."

"Ok then, on we go." Elaine went to the galley to get some fresh coffee.

When she returned a few minutes later, Tom had formulated a plan. "Do you think you can get me on the Crossline show?" he asked.

"You? The most wanted man in America? I think I can make that happen."

CHAPTER 44

"Ok, Tom, you are on in one minute. Webcam is ready and all of the video feeds from the factory are set," Elaine said. "Is Eric's code done?"

"Yes, he just put the finishing touches on it. All I have to do is enter my authorization key," Tom replied.

"Are you sure you want to do this, Tom? Adding fuel to the fire?"

"What's the worst that can happen? I'm already America's most wanted man," Tom joked. "Alright, here we go." The webcam went live and the split screen showed the Crossline host on one side and Tom on the other.

"Ladies and gentlemen, welcome to Crossline. Last night's show was big, and tonight's is even bigger. Our exclusive guest tonight, from international waters somewhere off the coast of North Carolina, is America's new most wanted man, Tom Jackson," Bob Jenkins said. "Let's get right to it."

"Welcome, Mr. Jackson. You've had quite a week – price gouging, contempt of Congress, ordering an illegal work slowdown, and now kidnapping. Your comments?"

"Thanks for having me on the show, Bob. I spent years in the US Navy intercepting pirates off the coast of Somalia. Pirates are called the scourge of mankind because they don't make anything themselves, they just steal what has been lawfully produced by others. But at least in Somalia the pirates have the guts to steal out in the open."

"Why am I now America's most wanted man? Because I took the risk to create and produce? Because I offered a product to customers at a price they agreed to pay? Because I built an enterprise that employs hundreds of people? And for this creative endeavor I am now the villain? What I created is now seized in order to control it, all under the umbrella of the law? Who are the real pirates now?"

Bob Jenkins interrupted, "But Mr. Jackson, what about providing light bulbs to the American people? Aren't they entitled to light? Isn't it a matter of national security?"

"Entitled? Of course not. Where did we get the idea that we are entitled to anything? All of these notions of entitlement are done in the name of leadership, of progress. Yet how can it be leadership if you are telling people that they do not have to think for themselves? That they do not have to produce? That they can properly live off of the labor and property of others? That they can get all manner of benefits for free, on borrowed money?"

Bob Jenkins was squirming, "That's quite a radical view, Mr. Jackson."

"Perhaps. But just look at the result. We've created a nation of infants. Infants who are not only dependent on the state for their every material need, but dependent on some authority to tell them what to do in any given situation. Infants who whine to pandering politicians every time the price of gas or anything goes up. And you call that progress?"

"Why not build up their self-reliance instead? So

instead of waiting for some day out in the future, why not start treating people like adults now? Why not tap into their innate entrepreneurial spirit? That is truly the big missing."

Bob Jenkins squirmed. The veteran anchor was at a loss for words.

Tom continued, "You can hold on to the notion that somehow the American people are entitled to all sorts of things, but my question to you is this – who's going to provide it?

"Right now, my loyal employees are working under so-called federal supervision – here you can see how they've become like zombies, going through the motions." Tom brought in the video feed of the factory.

"But tonight, I'm going to release them of that absurd obligation. I'm shutting down the factory's computer systems so that no more light bulbs will be produced. You may claim that the American people are entitled to bulbs, but they will get no more from me."

Tom made a few keystrokes, entering the activation code for the kill switch that Eric had developed over the past twenty-four hours. The software virus rippled through the factory's automation systems, inventory systems, financial systems, and every computer throughout TJ Enterprises. The video feed from the factory showed the production equipment lurch to a halt. The employees of TJ Enterprises stepped away from the production lines, and the factory floor was now silent, still, and empty.

CHAPTER 45

Atlantic Ocean

"Tom, you were awesome," Elaine said as she de-activated the webcam. "Did you really unleash a computer virus on your own factory systems?"

"Well, yes and no. The feds will spend countless hours trying to untangle the mess we created and absolutely nothing will work in the meantime. Brilliant piece of code from Eric. However, if and when we regain control of our property, we can be up and running in about an hour – we have a complete replica of our entire system stored in the cloud on a set of virtual servers. A couple of keystrokes and we are good to go."

Elaine didn't really understand the technical aspects, but seemed impressed that Tom and Eric had pulled it off so quickly.

Tom's concern was now much more immediate.

"It's only a matter of time now – they are closing in on us. Does Eric have anything yet on the sabotage investigation?"

"Nothing. But I know he's working on it."

"Alright, let's get some sleep. I get the feeling that tomorrow's going to be a crazy day. You get some rest; I'll take the first watch," Tom directed.

In the morning, Elaine kept trying to reach Eric – by phone, email, tweet, and text. "Eric – please help fast! We need some evidence or proof to clear Tom." But no luck. She was getting really nervous. Maybe the congressman was trying to give her a way out with the whole kidnapping ploy, but she was all in now. She'd spent enough time with Tom to begin to really appreciate his perspective. In fact, she was starting to grow quite fond of him. But now she knew that he was in real danger.

Elaine was pacing around the deck while Tom was up on the bridge. Finally her cell phone vibrated and chirped. She raced to pull it out of her pocket and was thrilled to see Eric's photo on the screen. She answered.

"Hey, nice work on the kill switch. I hate to pressure you, but we've got to get something to clear Tom. I've been trying to reach you for hours."

"Sorry, look I can't talk long. I don't have much time."

"What, you have a hot date?" Elaine joked.

"No, I think the feds are on to me. I've been poking around some places I shouldn't. But I think I've figured out who is behind the light bulb sabotage."

"Really? Great, what've you got?"

"I'm sending you some photos now. If they don't get to you, I've also posted them in our secret online location. Basically, I kept tracking the tweets and online postings about the CFL breakages," Eric explained. "They spread to the northeast and then died out. The total number of breakages is consistent with what you could ship in one container. So whoever stole the container, this was really all of their ammunition, so to speak."

"Ok, got it. Go on."

"Based on the tweet patterns, I was able to zero

in on the most likely stores in each area where the bulbs had been placed on shelves. Based on the time lag data, I created a crude algorithm to estimate when the bulbs were placed in the stores."

"Eric, where is this leading?"

"Sorry, keep with me. In case they get to me, I need someone else to know the story."

"What do you mean, get to you?" Elaine was getting worried.

"I can't explain now, but I think the same guys going after Tom are coming after me, once they figured out what I was on to. Look, we are running out of time," Eric's voice was tense.

"Ok, keep going," Elaine said.

"Here's where I started to get into get myself into trouble. These big stores all run surveillance video cameras covering their parking lots and stores. Old school approach was to keep VCR tapes for a few days and then record over them – but now all the video is digital and stored on remote servers. Since storage is so cheap, they keep it indefinitely. So I remotely accessed the digital video files for the stores in question, plus or minus two to three days from the estimate date of the bulb placement."

"By remotely accessed, you mean hacked."

"Technically speaking, yes. But here's the thing. I patched in top secret facial recognition software out of the National Security Agency and ran it against these videos. The algorithm's been running for a few days, going through hours of videos across several dozen stores."

"What are you looking for? Matches with criminal databases?"

"Not initially. At first, I'm just looking for people to show up at multiple places. So this facial recognition software creates a kind of numerical map of people's faces. It took some time to scan through hundreds of hours of video from multiple stores. But then it becomes pretty easy."

"Easy, how?"

"We now have a database of all of these people's numerical face maps and we search it for repeats. Sure enough, we got a hit – two individual face maps that somehow show up in multiple videos from stores across the country. Then we can go back to the actual video timestamps, pull the footage and see who they are. I'm sending you some screen capture photos now."

Elaine checked her email and saw a dozen or so images. Two guys, both with dark hair and a few days beard growth. In some they were in the parking lot, in others they were walking into or out of the stores in various places across the country.

"Wow, Eric, this is great. Any idea who these guys are?"

"Yes, here's where it gets bizarre, Elaine. Once I had these guys identified as being at the stores, I ran their photos against the national security photo databases that I have access to via my research grant. I had to age the photos, but we definitely have a match. We have older photos of them from Afghanistan and Iraq from several years ago, then nothing. They went off the grid a few years ago and haven't been seen since. These guys are both Al Qaeda. You get these photos yet?"

"Got em." Elaine confirmed. "So you are saying we have Al Qaeda operatives here in the US?"

"Not anymore."

"What do you mean, not anymore."

"Well, at least not these guys. I got a hit on these photos against another database. Next set of photos I'm sending you shows them separately exiting passport control at Dulles and Newark airports a couple of months ago. They're gone – and they could be anywhere in the world by now."

CHAPTER 46

Atlantic Ocean

Elaine ran up to the bridge and relayed her new intel from Eric. Tom wondered aloud, "Why in the world would Al Qaeda be behind this? What do they hope to accomplish?"

"No idea, but they certainly stirred up a bunch of chaos," Elaine said.

Tom and Elaine looked off the port side where a Coast Guard Patrol Boat was approaching from off in the distance. Tom continued his course south as they were about twenty nautical miles from Charleston.

Elaine was clearly getting nervous. "Tom, what are we going to do?"

"I'm not sure just yet."

"Look, Tom, we've got to get the story out about what's really going on. They are spinning the media to make people think you've kidnapped me and that you are behind the sabotage. We've got to get this story out."

As the Coast Guard boat approached, Tom decided to make radio contact. "Coast Guard Patrol, this is Tom Jackson, do you copy?"

"Copy, Mr. Jackson. Is Elaine Mitchell with you?

"Yes. She is here of her own free will."

"Look skipper, we don't know what to make of this, but we have orders to board your vessel, secure Ms. Mitchell, and arrest you."

Elaine tapped Tom, "Quick, do you have a dry bag?"

Tom looked puzzled, "Yes, check the bin over there. What are you doing?"

"Tom, if they capture you and me together, this story will never come out. You've got to make it back to Charleston. I'm a liability to you now."

"So what are you going to do?"

"I'm going to get back to shore and really get to

work. Get your boat ready to make your move. You've got to run for it." As she talked, she took her laptop and cellphone, wrapped them in plastic wrap, put them in the dry bag, then wrapped it over her shoulder and clipped it to her belt. Then she put on a life jacket.

Tom watched the Coast Guard vessel approach with the boarding party assembling on the deck. He edged the yacht a few degrees to the southeast, angling for a course of escape.

"Get ready, Tom. Follow my lead." Elaine led Tom from the bridge out to the deck. She waved to the Coast Guard vessel as it closed in. She leaned over to Tom, kissed him on the cheek, and then jumped overboard.

Tom watched the Coast Guard crew scramble on the deck as he walked back to the bridge of the yacht. He radioed the Coast Guard vessel, giving them the coordinates of his position. "You've got a civilian overboard. Please provide rescue support immediately."

Tom eased the throttle to get well clear of Elaine and then gunned the engines to run full out into the open sea. As he looked back through his binoculars, he saw a Coast Guard helicopter arrive on the scene, hovering overhead. They lowered a crewman via a cable who hooked Elaine into his harness and then they hoisted them both up to the helicopter deck.

Tom held his breath to see what the Coast Guard vessel would do next. Would it continue to come after him? He continued to increase distance, and then sighed in relief as he saw the Coast Guard vessel head in the opposite direction. He wasn't exactly sure why, but he was in the clear, at least for a little while.

CHAPTER 47

Tom was now alone again. This whole situation seemed to be spiraling out of control. All he wanted to do at this point was to return to his factory and stand with his employees who were now holding strong and refusing to work for their new federal supervisors.

And what to make of Elaine? Tom thought. Just a few days ago she painting me the villain and now she had just risked her life for me. Tom looked back again towards the Coast Guard vessels that were no longer visible on the horizon. How will I get to reconnect with her?

Tom pulled up the newsfeed on his flat panel screen and watched the unfolding events. News cameras from a helicopter showed the westbound lanes of Interstate 26 heading out of Charleston toward Columbia blocked by a slew of pick-up trucks and horse trailers strewn sideways. Just behind the blockade, a dozen 18-wheeler tractor trailers loaded with light bulbs sat motionless. From the aerial view, the eastbound lanes into Charleston were clear and moving freely.

A news reporter on the scene broke in and started talking, "Looks like we have some movement here. An apparent agreement has been reached for the 18-wheelers to return back to the plant. The pickups are moving out of the way and the trucks carrying light bulbs are exiting and then turning around to go back into Charleston."

Tom watched with a glimmer of hope as the news helicopter tracked the fleet of trucks moving. But when the trucks continued past the exit back to his plant, Tom's hopes quickly faded. Where were they headed now?

At that moment, Tom's phone rang and he answered quickly, "Please hold for the governor." Tom had been trying to reach the South Carolina governor for a couple of days.

The governor came on the line and got right down to business. "Well, I've gotta tell you, Mr.

Jackson, you've stirred up quite a mess. Sure, the price gouging charges are bogus, but industrial sabotage, kidnapping a reporter, and now obstruction of justice for the stunt you pulled to shut down your own plant? I know you are a citizen of my state, but I've got to help bring you in."

"Governor, I understand your position, but I don't think you have all the facts. Elaine Mitchell was with me of her own free will. The Coast Guard just picked her up about thirty minutes ago. As soon as she gets to shore, she's coming to see you with important evidence. Go meet with her and listen to her story. As for me, I'm coming back to my factory as soon as I can."

"Evidence of what?"

"That Al Qaeda terrorists were behind the CFL sabotage."

"Al Qaeda? Here in the U.S.?"

"Not any more. They are long gone."

The governor paused and then redirected, "Tom, do you hear how outrageous that story sounds? Given my situation, I've got to listen to the feds on this one."

"All I ask is that you listen to Elaine. And, since you are listening to the feds, where are they taking my trucks?"

"Back to your factory. I persuaded them to try to cool things off a bit. That was the agreement to get our citizens to clear out and allow the trucks to turn around. They saw the federal action as outright theft."

"Except that the feds driving my trucks just drove right past the exit. From what I'm seeing on the news, it looks like they are headed to the port."

"Dammit. We've been double-crossed!" The governor was now enraged.

"You're surprised? Looks like the feds plan to move the bulbs out by sea."

"Well, good luck with that. As soon as that plan gets out, I'm sure our citizens of South Carolina will never stand for that and will figure out how to block the port as well. Tom, I will go meet with Elaine and hear her out. Who the hell knows where this is headed now."

Tom continued south and watched the streaming news feeds en route. After a few minutes, the major news networks cut to an impromptu press conference in front of the port of Charleston.

The lighting czar was back on camera. "We are moving with all deliberate speed to get these light bulbs distributed to the public. We have a team of specialists working around the clock to get production up and running again. Unfortunately, our plan to transport bulbs by land was blocked by unruly protesters. But we cannot wait to get this critical supply restored, so we are going to transport by sea out of the port of Charleston. Just a quick trip up the coast to the port of Baltimore and we'll be able to distribute the bulbs to groups with critical needs – schools, agencies, and seniors on fixed incomes. Do not fear. We will have them to you shortly."

CHAPTER 48

Charleston, SC

Elaine Mitchell was soaking wet, but otherwise felt no worse for the wear after being pulled out of the ocean by the Coast Guard crew. Within minutes of jumping over the side of Tom's yacht, she was drying out under a large blanket as the helicopter headed to shore. She kept her dry bag close strapped to her waist under her clothes, protecting the evidence she carried. Maybe Eric had a copy, but she couldn't count on it.

Once the helicopter landed, Elaine was ushered into a small building. She observed a heated discussion occurring among the Coast Guard personnel before she was led into a small conference room. Were they detaining her? As far as she was concerned, along with the story in the press, Elaine was the hostage. She should be free to go.

After a few minutes, Elaine looked though the conference room window and saw a pair of South Carolina State Troopers walk into the building. A heated conversation ensued between the troopers and the Coast Guard personnel. Moments later, the door clicked open and one of the troopers spoke to Elaine, "Ms. Mitchell, would you come with us please? We'd like to speak with you outside."

Elaine was quite confused, but agreed. The troopers escorted her out of the building where a pair of patrol cars was waiting next to a black limousine. "What's going on?" Elaine asked one of the troopers.

"Ma'am, the Coast Guard wants to keep you here until the FBI can get your statement about Mr. Jackson. We convinced them that you might be able to help us bring him in, so they let you at least talk to us for a few minutes," the trooper answered.

"How? What are you talking about?"

"If you'll step into the limo, ma'am, you'll understand. We'll be right here."

Elaine looked back at the Coast Guard building, hesitated momentarily, and then turned and stepped into the car.

CHAPTER 49

Elaine was shocked to see the governor of South Carolina. "Hello, Ms. Mitchell. We could really use your help."

"Governor?" Elaine exclaimed, and then tried to recover. "Pardon my surprise. But can you please tell me what is going on?"

"Ms. Mitchell, I've been in communication with Tom Jackson. Do you have the photos that he told me about?"

Elaine was skeptical. Was the South Carolina governor working with the feds? If she handed it over, she'd have nothing and Tom would be screwed.

The governor read her expression, "May I call you Elaine?" She nodded. "I've known Tom a long time. He's a model citizen in these parts. He had me come visit his factory when it first opened. I was thrilled to see the new jobs coming here after all of the Boeing mess. I trust Tom and know that he wouldn't do anything that they are accusing him of, but I need some proof."

Elaine hesitated, "Governor, I appreciate your concern. But let's just say I'm extremely skeptical about cooperating with any government official right now."

"Well how about that," the governor laughed. "So now you're skeptical. I'm skeptical, too."

Elaine's expression was even more confused now. "I'm sorry, Governor. I don't understand."

The governor pulled out a laptop computer from his bag and handed it to Elaine. "I'm not asking you to trust me or to hand over your evidence. I'm suggesting you just put it out on the Internet so it becomes public. And if you really do have the evidence that Tom says you have, it will be the proverbial last straw."

"What do you mean, last straw?"

The governor pulled a manila file folder from a

briefcase. "This bill right here is awaiting my action. It passed the state legislature unanimously this morning in an emergency session. Either it gets a veto or it gets my signature. If you have proof that Al Qaeda was behind this CFL sabotage and the feds have been hiding it to go after Tom, then that really is the last straw. I'll sign it. This madness must stop."

"Sign what?" Elaine asked. The governor handed the folder to Elaine and watched her eyes bulge in shock as she opened it and read its contents. The large words at the top of the page said it all:

ARTICLES OF SECESSION.

We the people of the state of South Carolina hereby withdraw and secede from the United States of America and declare South Carolina to be a sovereign, independent nation.

"Elaine, people in this state are fed up with the feds. Pun intended. The feds jerk us around for years telling Boeing that they can't open a plant here. Hundreds of new jobs vanish in the meantime. Then Tom actually opens a plant, hires a couple hundred people, starts selling a legal product to people who want to buy it, and the feds come in and seize it. Now, if they are framing him for this sabotage and diverting attention from an Al Qaeda plot, that's just outrageous. And to think this all started because they want to dictate what kind of light bulbs we have to use."

Elaine was flabbergasted. "Can you actually do this? Secede, I mean. You can't just pack up and walk away."

"Look, Elaine. We hear all the time about how things are unsustainable in this country – debt, bailouts, entitlements, and polarized politics. If something is really unsustainable, then eventually it has to stop. Government derives its authority from the consent of the governed. The people of South Carolina have withdrawn our consent. Enough is enough."

Elaine looked away from the governor and stared out the window of the limo. She knew Tom was getting closer to Charleston but that the Coast Guard and Navy would be rapidly closing in on him. She had to get evidence out into the public to clear Tom's name. But doing so would trigger secession and maybe even a second civil war. Tears started streaming down her face.

The limo pulled away. "Elaine, I need you to make a decision. Think about it as we drive over to the site of the signing ceremony. "

"Where?" Elaine asked.

"Where else, Fort Sumter, of course."

CHAPTER 50

The same exact thought went through two separate minds at the exact same instant.

Captain Scott "Buzzsaw" McClendon maneuvered the F-16 Fighting Falcon along the taxiway of the McEntire Joint National Guard Base just outside of Columbia, South Carolina. After several tours in Iraq, Scott had left the Air Force and returned to his home in South Carolina where he flew commercially for US Airways out of Charlotte. He stayed active in the National Guard so he could maintain his flight hours. Besides, flying the F-16 was still a lot more fun than driving an Airbus. Scott opened up the throttle. The jet screamed down the runway and was airborne within seconds, heading towards Charleston.

Scott's squadron has been mobilized in the early

morning hours and he had to call in and cancel his work schedule. He was supposed to be flying a bunch of tourists from Charlotte down to Punta Cana in the Dominican Republic and then bringing another planeload back in the evening. Instead, he and eleven other planes were establishing a combat air patrol perimeter around Charleston – under orders from the governor. The governor was mobilizing South Carolina militia units all over the state in an effort to prevent the federal seizure of the Port of Charleston. Scott's F-16 had been armed with air-to-air sidewinder missiles as well as anti-ship missiles. And get this, he had clearly been told that this was not a drill.

Meanwhile, Lieutenant Perry Singleton pulled up on the controls of the Navy Seahawk helicopter and lifted off the back deck of the Arleigh-Burke Class Destroyer. The destroyer had been in port in Jacksonville, Florida after a deployment in the Indian Ocean when they were called out to sea yesterday morning. As the ship raced north towards Charleston, Perry's helo crew received their mission orders: intercept a racing yacht piloted by one Tom Jackson, Captain, USN Retired. Attempt capture. Destroy if necessary.

As the F-16 and Seahawk helicopter arrived over the Charleston harbor, the same thought went through the minds of both pilots simultaneously, "What the hell is going on?"

CHAPTER 51

Elaine rode in silence as the governor's limo navigated the streets of Charleston, heading to the ferry terminal to Fort Sumter National Monument. Her mind was a flurry of confusion. Fort Sumter?

"Governor, why Fort Sumter?"

"In 1861 at Fort Sumter, the first shots were fired in a deadly civil war that tore this nation apart. We were, as Abraham Lincoln said, 'a house divided'. We were divided over an abomination – the forced enslavement of fellow human beings on the basis of race. That war brought a decisive end to this horrific practice."

"So what divides us now?" Elaine asked. "Clearly it is not one big thing, but thousands of tiny small things. Thousands of tiny fractures. We go about our lives for years, never noticing these tiny encroachments. A regulation here, a regulation there. All in the name of progress. By themselves they seem so reasonable, even advisable. But we never seem to ask what each little incremental step costs us. Each little step removes a tiny bit of our liberty, so slowly that we do not notice it."

The governor laughed, "If I weren't looking right at you, I'd swear I was listening to Tom Jackson!"

Oh my God! Tom. Elaine's felt the turmoil in her mind ripple through her body. She looked out the window as tears started streaming down her face. What would Tom do? God, I hope he's ok. He's out there making his stand. Now it's my turn. The fate of the union is in my hands. Would she in fact be the one to release the last straw, enabling the governor's signature, and then perhaps bringing down the republic? Come on, Elaine, she told herself. Put your ego in check. Forces way bigger than just you are in motion here.

She looked back to the governor and tried to compose herself, "I always took it for granted that America would always exist. But based on what?"

"Great question, Elaine. You know, our founders

said 'enough' to King George in 1776. Are you surprised that finally the people are saying 'enough' now?"

Elaine sighed, "No, I guess I just realized that there's no law of the universe that says that the United States of America is permanent."

CHAPTER 52

In her last attempt at denial, Elaine stalled by opening the laptop and surfing to her favorite news sites to check the latest happenings. She scanned the headlines for updates on the crisis. Sure enough, the congressman was on video yet again, continuing to milk the crisis. She clicked on the video, which took a few minutes to buffer since they were in a moving vehicle. The governor looked on as she watched.

The congressman began, "My fellow Americans, I want to reassure you that we are doing everything within our power to restore the supply of light bulbs to the American people. Unfortunately, our efforts to transport these bulbs has been hampered by law-breaking individuals who seem intent on blocking us from moving these bulbs by land. We expect to have the Port of Charleston under control this morning and will begin shipping bulbs by sea this afternoon. Tom Jackson will be apprehended, brought to justice, and the production of light bulbs will resume."

"Where does it stop, Elaine?" the governor asked.

The time for delay was over, she realized. Elaine pulled the USB drive from the dry bag attached to her belt. It was dry and presumably safe. She inserted the flash drive and navigated to the folder with the series of photos that Eric sent. She clicked through them several times, trying to verify to herself that the photos did indeed provide the evidence she claimed.

The photo evidence was quite convincing. She turned to the governor and spent a few minutes going through the evidence. Yes, the governor agreed.

The governor's car stopped and they got out. They had arrived at the ferry port that provided transportation out to Fort Sumter. At the dock, a small contingent of troops from the South Carolina Guard as well as several more state troopers were waiting.

Elaine and the governor's party boarded, along with a couple of news reporters and camera crews from the local news stations. Elaine noticed the looks of surprise on the reporters' faces when they recognized her, yet the reporters were remarkably restrained.

The governor led Elaine up to the observation deck, where Elaine could now see the hundreds of small craft heading out into the harbor. "Oh my goodness, look at all of those boats! What are they doing?" she asked. Off in the distance, she could see hundreds of people lining the Cooper River Bridge looking out into Charleston Harbor.

"Elaine, our citizens have taken it upon themselves to blockade our own harbor to prevent the feds from moving the light bulbs out by sea. We've had enough. There are forces at play here much bigger than you. Don't think that by withholding your photo evidence that you can somehow keep this union together. Release the photos, Elaine, and let events run their course."

Elaine nodded and logged into her Twitter account. As her account came up on the screen, she watched the governor sign the Articles of Secession with a slow, trembling tragic arc of the pen.

Elaine's eyes welled up with tears as she composed what would later be called "the Tweet heard round the world." It took her a few minutes to get her message down to just 140 characters, the maximum permitted. "CFL sabotage by Al Qaeda, not Tom Jackson. Pics here. Feds stealing his property. South Carolina secedes -- says 'enough', we're outta here."

CHAPTER 53

Atlantic Ocean, near Charleston Harbor

"Thank you, Elaine!!!! Woooo hooo!" Tom shouted from the bridge to no one in particular. As he worked the controls of the yacht, Tom checked the major networks on his flat panel display. At first glance, all he saw was the photos of the Al Qaeda operatives being displayed. She'd made it to safety and the photos were out. At least I can clear my name, Tom thought.

But when the networks displayed the South Carolina state flag with a huge graphic banner saying "SC Secedes!," Tom did a double take. He had to slow the boat down enough and crank the volume to hear the reports over the sound of the wind as the yacht raced southward. Secession? It can't be. There must be a mistake.

While Tom's mind searched for answers, he realized he now had a much more imminent problem. He was rapidly running out of fuel, and a pair of Coast Guard vessels was converging on his position from the north, closing fast.

"Come on, baby, I just need a little more juice to get home," he pleaded with the yacht.

As he rounded the corner of Sullivan's Island and made the turn inland towards Charleston, Tom was shocked at the sight before him. The water was littered with the confetti of hundreds of small craft. Nearly every civilian vessel in the area – every sailboat, yacht, powerboat, and fishing boat – had all put out to sea to watch the festivities. How can the feds possibly get a large merchant vessel out of the harbor now?

Tom used his field glasses to check the position of the Coast Guard vessels. They were definitely closing in, and at this pace, he would not make it – he'd have to make a move soon. He kept on course and was now passing an increasing number of civilian boats as he approached the harbor. People were waving and cheering him on.

"Attention, Tom Jackson. This is the United

States Coast Guard. Stop and prepare to be boarded." Tom ignored the radio call from the vessel bearing down upon him.

The announcements of the Coast Guard were interrupted by a booming foghorn coming from the south. Tom looked up to see a large cruise ship approaching and raised his binoculars to check it out. The Carnival Fantasy – returning from its usual five-day trip to the Bahamas. Hundreds of passengers were lining the deck rails, marveling at the sight of hundreds of boats in front of them.

"Hmm. I wonder if the Carnival captain knows what's going on – but in any case, here's my chance," Tom said to himself. After years of hunting pirates, Tom decided to borrow a tactic from their playbook – just like the Somali pirates would circle the big merchant ships, Tom would cling close to the Carnival liner and seek cover into port.

Tom slowed slightly and pulled near a few of the civilian speedboats that were out at the edge of the harbor. Will they help me in this? We'll see. He indicated via hand signals that he planned to move ahead, and motioned back towards the Coast Guard ships. Tom wasn't sure if they knew what he had in mind, but as long as it was confusing and chaotic, it would buy him some time.

It seemed to work well enough. As Tom increased his speed and moved toward the cruise ship, a couple of speed boats turned north right into the paths of the Coast Guard vessels. Perfect. Just enough to cause them to slow and give Tom the time he needed to move close to the Carnival Fantasy. Tom gunned the engines and raced around the back of the wake, so that the cruise ship would be between him and the Coast Guard.

But what he saw next caused him to nearly faint.

As he cleared the Carnival Cruise ship, he saw a US Navy Arleigh Burke-class destroyer approaching from the south. They weren't kidding. Between hunting down Tom and taking control of the Port of Charleston, the feds had pulled out the big guns.

Tom cleared the wake and pulled alongside the Carnival Fantasy on its port side as it headed into the harbor. It was slowing down, clearly concerned about the massive logjam of civilian boats in the harbor.

The helicopters from the destroyer were approaching. Tom couldn't believe it. The very anti-piracy tactics that he'd developed were now being used against him. The helos circled as Tom pulled alongside the cruise ship. He knew they were acquiring laser targeting on him – but the ultimate question was would they fire?

The two helicopters took up positions at each end of the ship and Tom was now trapped in the middle. As long as Tom stayed close, he felt pretty safe – there was no way that they'd fire with him so close to the cruise liner.

The fuel warning light was now flashing. He was running on fumes now.

At that moment, one of the civilian boats out in the water tried to come close to Tom for a moment in the spotlight.

"Hey Tom, you rock, man! Give 'em hell!" A few guys raised their beers to toast Tom as they'd apparently decided to make a party out of the occasion.

"Hey, look out!" Tom shouted back as the small craft came dangerously close to the yacht.

To avoid the collision, Tom gunned the yacht and maneuvered out of the way before the small boat slammed into the cruise liner, sending a couple of guys overboard.

"Come on, let's roll!" Tom sensed that this was his moment and gunned the engines. He went all out toward Fort Sumter, weaving in and out of the boats in his way.

Tom looked up overhead to see the Navy helicopters in hot pursuit, flanking him on either side. "Just a few seconds more...." he pleaded. At this speed, he was kicking up a huge spray which splashed up over the sides of the yacht. He looked ahead, seeing a large crowd of people assembled on the outer walls of Fort Sumter.

Off in the distance, Elaine stood alongside the governor on the eastern-most point of the wall of Fort Sumter and watched in horror as the helicopters circled Tom's yacht. She felt totally helpless. The governor looked through binoculars, narrating the action. "Looks like the Navy is trying to circle Tom's boat, getting ready to fire. We'll see if our F-16s can cause some kind of diversion." The governor relayed the order.

A few moments later, Elaine watched a pair of F-16s fighter jets from the South Carolina Guard buzz low across the harbor, cutting right between Tom and the Navy helicopter. But it was not enough. The Navy helicopter backed off slightly, but quickly regained its angle. With the laser target still active, the destroyer fired. Seconds later, the missile entered the water just behind the Tom's boat. A huge plume of water erupted from behind Tom's boat. Elaine screamed in horror.

The large charge exploded just behind Tom's yacht. The force of the blast knocked Tom off his feet and he slammed into the deck.

Everything went black.

CHAPTER 54

Fort Sumter, South Carolina

When he came to after a few seconds, Tom felt groggy. He reached up to feel a big knot on the side of his head and the stickiness of blood. Other than a gash along his head, he seemed ok. He pulled himself up by a railing and noticed that the yacht was listing to one side. Tom tried to orient himself and looked around the boat. A Coast Guard vessel was fast approaching.

The blast had knocked out one engine, but the other engine was still functional. Even with one engine, he could make pretty decent speed. Tom looked around – he couldn't make it too far, but the Fort Sumter monument was just ahead. He cranked up the one remaining engine and turned the yacht straight towards the ferry pier at the national monument site.

Tom got just enough of a head start on his new course to outrun the Coast Guard. Apparently they thought they were approaching a stalled yacht, so when Tom turned up the engines, they were not expecting it. This split-second delay gave Tom just enough time to approach the pier, where mobilized South Carolina troops had established a position. The Coast Guard backed off, not wanting to draw any further escalation.

As Tom pulled up to the pier, the ferry crew helped secure his yacht. "Man, you just outran the damn U.S. Navy!" A young crewman gave Tom a hand as he stepped over the side onto the pier. The crew cheered and guided Tom to a waiting jeep.

Tom smiled and said, "Yeah, I guess I beat them at their own game. Great to be back on dry land."

A jeep came racing down the long pier from the fort itself and came to a stop about twenty feet in front of Tom. Elaine Mitchell jumped out of the passenger side and came running up to Tom. With cameras watching and broadcasting the entire event, she threw her arms around him. "My God, Tom, I thought you were dead!"

Tom and Elaine got into the jeep which sped down the long bridge from the pier to the tiny island of Fort Sumter, through the gate, and up unto the main parade grounds of the Fort. The governor waved from the platform where dozens of troops milled around.

Tom exited the jeep and looked around the fort. Something was not quite right. He'd visited the fort many times as a young boy and sailed past it hundreds of times. Other than the obvious fact that the tiny island was swarming with military troops from the South Carolina Guard and that a couple of helicopters were parked on the parade grounds, sure. But what was it?

Then it hit him. A large pole rose from the center of the fort, towering above the low-lying fortifications.

The American flag was gone.

CHAPTER 55

Philadelphia, PA, Three Months Later

"Tom, relax, you'll do great. Here, let me check your tie." Elaine blocked Tom from pacing so she could straighten his tie and brush some lint off of his suit.

The 100 Watt War, as the media was now calling it, had indeed consisted of one single shot fired, with no casualties other than the loss of a very expensive racing yacht.

Now, three months later, all fifty state governors were gathered in the convention hall of the Philadelphia Convention Center. Not just the fifty governors, but thousands of legislators from every state. While they couldn't replicate the original meeting space of the 1787 Constitutional

Convention, the modern convention center did have its advantages. For one, it could accommodate many thousands more people. And it had air conditioning.

Now, Tom Jackson, the man who'd been the target of that shot, paced in his hotel room as he prepared to address the convention. In the aftermath of the crisis, Tom had been the voice of reason, helping the governor of South Carolina to stand down, by insisting on a constitutional convention to address fundamental questions of United States governance, federalism, the constitution, and the republic itself.

"Are you ready?" Elaine checked her lipstick one last time.

Tom put his notes in his inside pocket, "Ready as I'll ever be."

Tom and Elaine walked to the elevator and rode down in silence. As they walked through the lobby and towards the convention floor, Elaine stopped Tom just short of the stage entrance.

"You know, Tom, there's a lot of talk."

"About what?"

"About you as President. The country needs a

leader. I've heard people from both parties who want to draft you."

Tom laughed, "Well, that is quite a compliment, but we'll have to take things one step at a time. For now, I'm not even sure what the country will look like – or if we'll have one at all."

"What do you mean?"

"It's hard to explain, but in a weird way, I'm actually somewhat comforted by the fact that our biggest battle comes from within. Our country is not being torn apart by a foreign invader and subjected to the occupation of a foreign power. Once again we have to determine for ourselves what freedom means and how to ensure it for future generations. It is my great hope that we can restore our original promise, but if that's not the case and we have irreconcilable differences among the states, then so be it. I'd rather have freedom that actually means something than try to just smooth things over. We've got major issues to resolve."

The noise from the convention floor started to swell as the announcer introduced Tom.

He started to walk out onto the platform when he did a double-take back towards Elaine, "Besides,

Elaine, for me to be President, I'd need something. Something rather important."

"What's that?"

Tom winked at her, "A first lady."

Is There More? An Invitation from the Author

The story of *The 100 Watt War* ends here, but the conversation is just getting started. Please visit www.The100WattWar.com where you can join the conversation on *The 100 Watt War* blog, leave your comments, and tell me what you think. I look forward to meeting you there.

At the site, you can also listen to an audio interview with me about *The 100 Watt War* to learn more about why I wrote this book, the story behind the story, and what's on my mind about economic freedom, entrepreneurship, and the role of government and business in our society. You can also find out about upcoming speaking events and book signings where we can meet in person. Check it out at www.The100WattWar.com.

See you there!

Ron Wilder

About the Author

Ron Wilder serves as a strategic advisor, coach, and teacher to business leaders worldwide. Ron works with CEOs, business owners, executives, entrepreneurs, and experts – in companies ranging in size from one-person start-ups to Fortune 500 corporations.

In 2003, Ron founded Aligned Action, a strategy-focused executive coaching and advisory firm. In Ron's work with clients, he assists leaders in creating big opportunities, taking the seeds of a vision and crafting a strategy to realize it, and aligning the organization to accelerate sales growth and profitability. Ron's work is typically behind-the-scenes, such that these results occur *through the leader* who is rapidly developing into a much more effective and powerful leader in the process.

Ron's career began in Silicon Valley, where he worked with R.B. Webber & Company, a boutique strategy consultancy and venture capital firm. He held sales, marketing, and corporate development roles for two venture-backed start-ups (one acquired by Yahoo!)

Ron holds a B.S. in Physics from Emory University and a M.S. in Engineering-Economic Systems from Stanford University. He served in the U.S. Naval Reserve and deployed to the Persian Gulf during Operation Desert Storm.

Ron enjoys playing classical piano and is an active practitioner and student of the martial arts, including Hapkido, Tai Chi, and Brazilian Jiu Jitsu. He lives outside of Raleigh, North Carolina with his wife and two daughters.

Ron writes extensively on business and leadership at his blog, found at www.alignedaction.com.

ACKNOWLEDGEMENTS

Thanks to my friends and clients who provided input and feedback on this book. Special thanks to Anne Braudy, for everything she does to support my work in the world; my editor-in-chief (and wonderful wife) Hardin Engelhardt; Steve Chandler for his extensive coaching; Richard Averitt; Randy Wilder; and of course, "my girls" -- Lacy, and Amelia – you are the best.

REFERENCES

Taleb, Nassim Nicholas. *The Black Swan: The Impact of the Highly Improbable*. New York: Random House, 2007.

Friedman, Milton. *Capitalism and Freedom: Fortieth Anniversary Edition*. Chicago: The University of Chicago Press, 2002, originally published in 1962.

Von Mises, Ludwig. *Human Action: A Treatise on Economics*. Auburn, Alabama: Ludwig von Mises Institute, 2010.

www.ingramcontent.com/pod-product-compliance
Lightning Source LLC
Chambersburg PA
CBHW061324170626
46817CB00001B/295